Palgrave Studies in Sub-National Governance

This series explores the formal organisation of sub-national government and democracy on the one hand, and the necessities and practices of regions and cities on the other hand. In monographs, edited volumes and Palgrave Pivots, the series will consider the future of territorial governance and of territory-based democracy; the impact of hybrid forms of territorial government and functional governance on the traditional institutions of government and representative democracy and on public values; what improvements are possible and effective in local and regional democracy; and, what framework conditions can be developed to encourage minority groups to participate in urban decision-making. Books in the series will also examine ways of governance, from 'network governance' to 'triple helix governance', from 'quadruple' governance to the potential of 'multiple helix' governance. The series will also focus on societal issues, for instance global warming and sustainability, energy transition, economic growth, labour market, urban and regional development, immigration and integration, and transport, as well as on adaptation and learning in sub-national government. The series favours comparative studies, and especially volumes that compare international trends, themes, and developments, preferably with an interdisciplinary angle. Country-by-country comparisons may also be included in this series, provided that they contain solid comparative analyses.

Steve Leach • Colin Copus

The Strange Demise of the Local in Local Government

Bigger is Not Better

palgrave
macmillan

Steve Leach
De Montfort University
England, UK

Colin Copus
De Montfort University
England, UK

ISSN 2523-8248 ISSN 2523-8256 (electronic)
Palgrave Studies in Sub-National Governance
ISBN 978-3-031-32818-3 ISBN 978-3-031-32819-0 (eBook)
https://doi.org/10.1007/978-3-031-32819-0

This Palgrave Macmillan imprint is published by the registered company Springer Nature Switzerland AG.
The registered company address is: Gewerbestrasse 11, 6330 Cham, Switzerland

To the memory of Professor John Stewart (1927–2022): an inspiration to the two authors and to countless academics, councillors and practitioners.

Acknowledgements

The book is dedicated to the memory of Professor John Stewart, who died in November 2022 at the age of 93. John was an inspiring scholar and teacher whose enthusiasm for local government and readiness to challenge the dominant role of central government inspired many thousands of local government practitioners and the academic staff who worked with him at the Institute of Local Government Studies. Both of us acknowledge the profound influence he has had on our thinking and on our careers and count ourselves fortunate to have worked with him. We are confident that he would have approved of the content of our book, which reflects his own long-term concerns about the overriding power of the centre.

We would also like to take the opportunity to thank others who have played an important part in our academic life: in Steve's case Professors David Wilson, Vivien Lowndes and Chris Skelcher, Professor George Jones, now sadly deceased, and Chris Game; in Colin's case, as well as recognising the part in his academic life of those mentioned, would also like to acknowledge and thank the late Professor Ken Young (his PhD supervisor and the man responsible for setting Colin on an academic career). Colin would also like to specifically acknowledge the influence on his career of the late Professor George Jones and Ken who were great mentors, colleagues and friends.

Steve would like to thank Councillors Martin Griffiths and James Hakewill of North Northamptonshire and Tom Beattie, former leader of Corby Borough Council, for helping him understand the machinations of the local government reorganisation in Northamptonshire in 2018.

Thanks also go to Councillor Giles Archibald, Westmorland and Furness Council, for his insights into the local government reorganisation in Cumbria.

We would also both like to thank the numerous councillors and local government officers we have taught, listened to and conversed with over the years. They have collectively provided a solid bedrock of understanding of the real world of local government, which has proved invaluable in our various publications.

Finally, we are grateful to our wives, Karen and Julia, for their support, tolerance and patience when we were writing this book (and on many former such occasions). What would we do without you!

Contents

1 Setting the Scene 1

2 The Way Things Used to Be 9

3 Reorganisation, Reorganisation, Reorganisation: The Changing Map of Local Government 19

4 Explaining the Persistence of the Unitary Principle in the Department's Mindset 37

5 A Strange Affair: Local Government Reorganisation in Northamptonshire 2018–21—A Case Study 47

6 Doomsday Approaches and then Recedes 61

7 What Is the Problem About Two-Tier Local Government? 73

8 Why Bigger Is Not Better 83

9 Where Do We Go from Here? 109

Appendix: How Devolution Based on Subsidiarity Might Work in England 123

Index 127

List of Figures

Fig. 8.1 Efficiency, effectiveness and performance: size doesn't matter 85
Fig. 8.2 Local democracy: size does matter 85

List of Tables

Table 7.1 Tiered sub-national/local government systems 79
Table 8.1 Average representative ratios 88
Table 8.2 The number of municipalities, the total number of councillors and the average number of councillors per council 89

CHAPTER 1

Setting the Scene

Abstract Over the past 50 years, local government in England has been progressively losing its link to the places and communities which matter to local people and with which they identify. This scenario is a matter of real concern and constitutional significance. Explaining how it has come about and highlighting its negative consequences are the main themes of the book. One outcome of the trend has been the increasing average size of local authorities in England, which is now over ten times greater than any European comparator. The 'bigger is better' argument, favoured by successive governments, which has led to the disappearance from the local government map of many 'real places', such as Barrow and Carlisle in Cumbria, is premised on the view that local authorities are merely agencies for service delivery, when in principle they should be seen as proactive governmental agencies, meeting the needs of local communities, as epitomised by the term 'place-shaping'.

Keywords Local government • Local democracy • Local government size • Local government structure • Local government reorganisation • Place-shaping • Community identity

Our starting point is the observation—which we defy anyone to dispute—that local government in England, over the past 50 years, has been

S. Leach, C. Copus, *The Strange Demise of the Local in Local Government*, Palgrave Studies in Sub-National Governance,
https://doi.org/10.1007/978-3-031-32819-0_1

progressively losing its link with the places and communities which matter to residents and with which they identify. Real places and communities are no longer seen as important considerations when changing local government structures by those who control the shape and boundaries of our councils. Local government areas in England (and indeed in Wales and Scotland too) have become effectively de-localised, a process which has progressed by stealth since 1992.

This observation leads to several important questions which our book addresses. What have been the impetus and rationale behind the de-localisation of local government? How convincing and evidence-based have been the arguments which have been deployed? Who benefits from the process? And does it really matter? Surely, local authorities, however designed or transformed, have always got on with the job and fulfilled their responsibilities at least (with very few exceptions) adequately?

We would be the first to acknowledge that local government structure is rarely high on the national political agenda and rarely does it capture the interest of large swathes of the population. But our view is that it does matter; indeed, it is a topic of profound importance. Local authorities constitute the only other level of elected government in England outside Westminster and Whitehall. It is a crucial element of our (unwritten) constitution. It has an important role of 'checks and balances' on central government power, not easy to exercise in the current climate, but vital in constitutional terms.

Most of the (largely futile) debate about the optimum size for local authorities has focused on their role in providing public services (planning control, waste collection, social care etc.). But local government is not just a vehicle for service provision. It is equally importantly a vehicle for local democracy and political and civic engagement. It is (or should be) a mechanism through which political views can be expressed and operationalised, including views at variance with those of the centre. The local governance role—the identification and implementation of strategic priorities for an area which transcend service provision responsibilities—has come to be known as 'place shaping', a term introduced in the influential Lyons report on the Future of Local Government (2007).

If the role of 'place shaping' is to be taken seriously, as we are clear it should be, then the move to large authorities, involving the amalgamation of real places undoubtedly hinders the process. The recent creation, from the county and districts of Cumbria, of two new unitary authorities—Cumberland Council and Westmorland and Furness Council—provides a telling illustration. Cumberland is an amalgamation of Carlisle, Allerdale and Copeland councils; Westmorland and Furness Council an amalgamation of Eden (focused on Penrith), South Lakeland (focused on Kendal) and Barrow-in-Furness.

Barrow-in-Furness is without doubt a real place with its own distinctive shipbuilding-based history and culture and its isolation from other parts of the county (the adjacent remainder of Furness excepted). Here, there is a clear basis for 'place-shaping' for an area and authority with real meaning for its inhabitants. How likely is it that a new council, created from an arbitrary portion of the former county, will inspire identity and loyalty on the part of its inhabitants? Very unlikely, in our view. Place-shapers here will have a frustrating and well-nigh impossible task, as they will with Cumberland council. No problem about place-shaping in the city of Carlisle, a place that is already well shaped! But the new unitary authority links it with a series of coastal towns with histories of coal mining, steel-making and seaport activity, with which Carlisle has very little in common, economically, socially or historically. Good luck, place-shapers you'll need it!

In relation to the current government's preoccupation with identifying an 'ideal size' for local authorities, the observation by Keating (1995) is similar to our own view:

> The 'right' size for a municipal government is a matter of local circumstances and the value judgement of the observer. Like so many issues in politics, this involves matters of ideology and interest

To which Newton (1982) adds:

> The search for optimum size has proved to be as successful as the search for the philosophers' stone, since optimality varies according to service and type of authority.

If community identity (whether 'affective' or 'effective' see Chap. 8) is taken into account (as it should be), there is a case for a unitary Rutland (population 40,000) just as there is for the now-abolished Strathclyde regional authority (population 2.5 million) though not, we hasten to add, for a unitary (all-purpose) Strathclyde.

Whether or not this or some future government conjures up some 'ideal size' from the ether, the long-held though unsubstantiated assumption that 'bigger is better' has dominated the thinking of successive governments (and in particular, the local government unit within the Department of Levelling Up, Housing and Communities (DLUHC) and its many predecessors) over the past 30 years. While it is acknowledged that local government in some other European countries has experienced reorganisation, involving amalgamations of existing authorities, the sheer scale of the resulting councils in England is unprecedented. Set out below are some data and comparisons which illustrate this point:

- In 2008, the average size of lower-tier (principle) authorities in England was 177,700, over ten times greater than four comparable European countries (France, Spain, Germany and Italy—see Council of Europe Committee on Local and Regional Democracy (CARD) (2008))
- Currently there are 87 unitary (all-purpose) authorities in England (assuming one includes the 36 metropolitan district councils which operate in conjunction with conurbation-wide Combined Authorities headed by an elected mayor). Elsewhere in Europe, countries operate an across-the-board two- or three-tier system of local government, with the exception of Latvia and Slovenia (Moreno, 2012).
- The recently designated unitary council of North Yorkshire has a population of 618,052. The USA state of Wyoming has a population of 579,495. Within it, there are 23 counties and 99 incorporated municipalities consisting of cities and towns within the state.
- North Yorkshire's area is 1.9 million acres, double that of the USA state of Rhode Island (989,000 acres). Rhode Island has 39 incorporated municipalities including 8 cities and 31 towns.

Although this book focuses primarily on local government in England, it is worth noting that Scotland and Wales operate systems equally out of line with those in Europe and the USA. Scotland's average local authority size is 186,000 and that of Wales, 140,990. Both countries consist wholly of unitary authorities (a model shared with Latvia and Slovenia (see above)). In Scotland the unitary Highland Council administers an area of 6.6 million acres, seven times larger than that of the state of Rhode Island.

The already vast discrepancy between average local authority size in England, the rest of Europe and in the USA is in danger of being extended even further. Early in 2020, the newly elected Conservative government announced plans for yet another local government reorganisation in the shire counties of England in which the two-tier system still existed. The initiative claimed to be a contribution to the prime minister's 'levelling up' agenda, although it was never explained how such a reorganisation might contribute to this goal. It soon became clear that the outcome the government had in mind was one involving the total abolition of the two-tier system and the introduction of large unitary councils, based on counties or part-counties. The then local government minister, Simon Clarke (who briefly returned to the ministry under the Truss government) expressed in February 2020 the view that the population of the new unitary authorities should be between 300,000 and 450,000, but that 'no upper limit should be imposed' (see Chap. 6 for further details). Mercifully this initiative was dropped when the scale of the Covid epidemic became apparent, but it is not unlikely that it will reappear, when the time is felt to be right.

If this proposal had been implemented on the basis of the size range specified, it would have reduced the number of local authorities in England from 318 (existing in 2023) to around 200, increasing the average size to around 290,000, nearly six times higher than the 1972 average. If the 'no upper limit' criterion were to be applied and the prospect of a unitary Surrey or Hertfordshire, both with populations close to 1,200,000 were to become a reality (although surely not Lancashire, Kent, Essex and Hampshire, all with populations over 1.3 million—but see Chap. 8 for an alternative view!) then the mismatch between the approach in England and that elsewhere in Europe would become even more glaring.

At the heart of the analysis which runs through the book is a debate about two competing narratives and visions for local government. The first—the technocratic view—sees local government primarily (and in some cases exclusively) as a mechanism for the provision of public services. The second—the governmental view—sees local government as an institution of local community-based self-governance, which focuses not only on service provision, but on community engagement and cohesion, strategic vision and the quality of local democracy. In the eyes of successive national governments (and their civil service advisors) it is clearly the technocratic view which prevails. Indeed, in these circles, this view has become the conventional wisdom, which appears to be blind to the alternative and resistant to any challenge to their assumptive world. It might be helpful if they were more aware of the history of local government: the proactive provision of gas, electricity and sewerage systems in Joseph Chamberlain's Birmingham: the cradle to grave health care policies of Alfred Salter's Bermondsey (Brockway, 1949) and (more recently) the transformation of the city centres and inner residential areas of cities like Manchester, Leeds and Newcastle. This is what the term 'local government' implies: furthering the economic, social and environmental well-being of its citizens, not merely operating as an agency for the provision or oversight of a specified range of public services, increasingly constrained by targets or standards set by central government. For this more limited role, it is not even clear that the elaborate political machinery which operates in local authorities is needed.

As we will argue later in the book, if it is the technocratic view of local government which is adopted, then arguments about economies of scale of service provision tend to dominate, typically leading to a 'bigger is better' conclusion. A review of the available evidence does not, however, support this conclusion. The research is inconclusive regarding the beneficial effects of increasing size. But if the governmental view is adopted then the evidence is crystal clear. As authority size increases, so are a whole range of indicators of democratic health adversely affected, including electoral turnout, public trust in councillors and officers, and levels of public engagement. And in a genuinely governmental system, the importance of basing authorities on places which have meaning and significance for local people becomes a consideration of equal if not more importance than (unproven) economies of scale.

The structure of the book is as follows: in Chap. 2, we explore the concepts of 'place' and 'community' and argue that these ideas remain important reference points for large numbers of people. The importance of the link between identification with place and the definition of local authorities is highlighted. We go on to look back to a time, less than 50 years ago, when there was a much closer fit between settlements with a strong local identity and local authority boundaries than there is now; a congruence not dissimilar to the French communes, which are still providing this vital local dimension.

There follows in Chap. 3 a review of the sequence of local government reorganisations in England since 1974 and how this has progressively undermined the link between place and local authority, to the extent that local government can hardly any longer be regarded as 'local'. In this process, a conventional wisdom has developed at the centre that 'bigger is better' and that the way forward is to dismantle the two-tier system wherever possible and to replace it with large unitary (all-purpose) authorities. It is this view which the book seeks to challenge.

In Chap. 4, we seek to provide an explanation of what has motivated this perspective, hypothesising that, given the lack of political salience of local government reorganisation on national political agendas, an explanation centred on the policy preferences of the civil service department which advises ministers in the DLUHC is the only plausible interpretation of events. A brief case study of the recent reorganisation in Cumbria is used to illustrate our argument.

A more detailed reorganisation case study follows in Chap. 5, detailing the bizarre circumstances in which the financial crisis in Northamptonshire County Council in 2018 was used by the government as a justification for the abolition of the county and the seven constituent district councils and their replacement by two unitary authorities: North and West Northamptonshire.

In Chap. 6 we explore the 'doomsday scenario' which emerged shortly after the Conservative election victory in 2019, which promised to scrap the two-tier system throughout the remaining shire counties where it remained and the reasons why it was largely discarded (or, more likely, postponed) when the scale of the Covid epidemic became clear.

Chapter 7 examines the case for the claim by successive governments that the two-tier system is dysfunctional and has passed its sell-by date and compares English predispositions and practice with that elsewhere in Europe, where two-tier (or indeed three-tier) systems of local government predominate and are rarely viewed as problematical. Research on the success of inter-authority collaboration in England and in Europe, both between and within tiers, and the scope for its extension are highlighted.

There follows in Chap. 8 a review of the vast array of academic evidence from England and elsewhere pertaining to the 'bigger is better' myth, drawing a key distinction between arguments regarding economies of scale of service provision and arguments about the impact of sizeism on the quality of local democracy and local community identity.

In Chap. 9, we suggest alternative policies which would combat what we see as the calamitous drift to a further increase in the number of large unitary authorities, a development which we argue would totally undermine the importance of the 'local' in local government.

The authors have sought to draw on the full range of academic evidence to give weight to this critique. But they also wish to provide a narrative which could be read from start to finish. As a result, they have sought to avoid including in the text the level of detail which would impede the flow and the impact of the narrative. In consequence, the evidence is summarised and illustrated in the text. But our arguments and the conclusions we draw are based on decades of international, independent academic research and evidence. While, we have referenced our arguments with that material throughout, the reader wishing to explore that evidence in more detail is referred to two reports produced by the authors: Copus et al. (2020), 'Bigger Is Not Better' and Copus (2022) 'Bigger Is Still Not Better'.

This is an important journey. Please share it with us.

References

Brockway, F. (1949). *Bermondsey story: The life of Alfred Salter*. Allen and Unwin.

Copus, C., Leach, S., & Jones, A. (2020). *Bigger is not better: The evidenced case for keeping 'local' government*. District Council's Network report.

Copus, C. (2022). *Bigger is still not better*. District Council's Network report.

Keating, M. (1995). Size, efficiency and democracy: Consolidation, fragmentation and public choice. In D. Judge, G. Stoker, & H. Wolman (Eds.), *Theories of urban politics* (pp. 117–134). Sage.

Lyons, M. (2007). *Lyons inquiry into local government: Final report*. The Stationery Office.

Moreno, A.-M. (2012). *Local government in the EU: A comparative legal perspective*. National Institute of Public Administration.

Newton, K. (1982). Is small really so beautiful? Is big really so ugly? Size, effectiveness and democracy in local government. *Political Studies, 30*(2), 190–206.

CHAPTER 2

The Way Things Used to Be

Abstract The concepts of 'place' and 'community' continue to provide important points of reference for large numbers of local people, as illustrated by the intensity of support for local football teams as 'symbols of place' and for other local institutions. The links between strong community identity and effective local government remain important, despite having been eroded by successive centrally imposed reorganisations. As recently as 1972, the local government map of England represented a much closer fit between strong local identity and local authority definition than it does at present, a situation not dissimilar to the French communes. Towns with populations as small as 5000 were represented by a local council and allocated responsibilities commensurate with their size. This model had and still has much to commend it.

Keywords Two-tier system • Unitary councils • London government • Place-shaping • Reorganisation • Community • Councillors • Localism • Subsidiarity • Local identity

Introduction

In this chapter we explore how much more closely tied English local government used to be to places and communities and examine how the fabric of local government was woven much more tightly into notions of

S. Leach, C. Copus, *The Strange Demise of the Local in Local Government*, Palgrave Studies in Sub-National Governance,
https://doi.org/10.1007/978-3-031-32819-0_2

community of place; a fabric that has progressively unravelled over time. It was in the late 1960s and early 1970s that a 'tipping point' can be identified, when a centralist attitude to local government became firmly established. It has continued ever since. Amongst its constituent elements have been a concern about local government structure and a growing belief that we need fewer, larger local authorities, a belief that we challenge throughout this book.

The next section of the chapter—an examination of 'how things used to be'—illustrates that there is an alternative to the continuing process of council abolitions and amalgamations. We go on to examine why the concepts of locality and place should be crucial in any consideration of local government structure and why they should provide a logical foundation for any local government reorganisation, rather than the current government's futile search for an optimum size for local government, which can be likened to an (equally fruitless) search for the 'philosophers' stone'. Such a perspective undermines community cohesion, and ultimately the legitimacy of how we are governed locally. The chapter concludes by drawing together the main lessons for the role of place in local government.

Local Government Structure: An Historical Perspective

It is important to remember that as recently as 1973, there was, throughout England, a congruence between the definition of local authorities and the places in which people lived and worked and with which they identified. The various Local Government Acts of the 1880s and 1890s had created a flexible system for achieving this outcome and for dealing with the different requirements of rural and urban governance (Chandler, 2007). County boroughs were introduced by the 1888 Local Government Act and initially required a population of 50,000 to justify an area being designated a 'county borough'. That qualifying population figure was increased to 75,000 in 1926 and to 100,000 in 1958. Claims for county borough status generated much conflict between county councils and what would then be municipal boroughs created since 1835. But it did mean that large towns and cities such as Liverpool and Birmingham on being granted county borough status were empowered to provide the full range of services which had been allocated to local government, similar to what today are called by the ahistorical term 'unitary councils' (see the next chapter for the origins of this term). As the extent of their built-up areas expanded, towns which grew markedly in size over the subsequent 70 years could apply to become county boroughs, with extended boundaries, and many did so, usually successfully.

Outside the county boroughs, a two-tier system of local government operated (three-tier, if parish councils are included). The traditional counties were responsible for what came to be known as the strategic functions (such as transportation and highways planning) and for those personal services deemed to require a relatively large population to operate effectively (such as education). Within the county areas were to be found municipal borough councils (MBCs), urban district councils (UDCs) and rural district councils (RDCs), all of which provided a range of local services. MBCs and UDCs were based on towns of varying sizes: all of them representing 'real places'. The functions for which they were responsible varied. The larger towns which had been designated MBCs were allocated a wider range than the UDCs, including in some cases a devolved responsibility for education. RDCs tended to lack the focus of MBs and UDs, typically comprising a scattering of smaller towns and villages. But all these different types of authority were small-scale in area and homogenous enough socially and economically, to prove meaningful to local people. And at the most localised level, there were the parish councils. It all sounds unduly complex and messy; but in fact, it represented a flexible interpretation of the principle of subsidiarity (although that was not an expression used at the time): the allocation of service responsibilities to the most local feasible territorial level.

In London, a two-tier system was also established around the same time. The London County Council was inaugurated in 1888 with broadly the same range of functions as the provincial county councils. In 1894, 28 London Boroughs were established, with functions similar to those of the MBCs. Most of these borough councils were based on the widely recognised 'London villages', places with powerful individual histories, celebrated in popular culture: places like Lambeth, Bethnal Green (see Young and Wilmott, 1957), Bermondsey (Brockway, 1949), Paddington, Hampstead and Stepney: and those with football club associations such as Tottenham, Chelsea and Fulham.

In the Greater Manchester area, where one of the authors worked in the 1960s, there were a total of 69 councils: 8 county boroughs, 16 municipal borough councils, 42 urban district councils and 3 rural district councils, operating (the CBs apart) within large areas of Lancashire and

Cheshire County Councils. For example, in what is now known as Tameside, there were ten separate authorities, all representing small- to medium-sized towns each with their own distinctive histories and cultural identities, fierce local loyalties and in several cases, much-loved football teams: Ashton-under-Lyne, Stalybridge, Hyde, Dukinfield, Audenshaw, Mossley and Droylsden. Reading the pages of the Tameside Advertiser in 2012, there were copious references to all these real places but very little mention of Tameside, apart from the activities of 'the council'. Elsewhere in Greater Manchester, the identities of townships with populations as small as 5000 were recognised in the existence of the urban districts of Lees (close to Oldham), Little Lever (between Manchester and Bolton) and Wardle (north of Rochdale). In the more rural parts of England, every market town with a population of 5000 or more (indeed sometimes less) had its own local authority to respond to its needs. In Cheshire, Alderley Edge (now home to various millionaire Manchester-based footballers), Knutsford (immortalised in Elizabeth Gaskell's Cranford), Winsford, Middlewich, Holmes Chapel and Sandbach all featured on the local government map. In such places, it was likely that you would know your local councillor personally, rather than, as now, having to check his or her access details on the internet. Local democracy was alive and well and living in Alderley Edge. The system was not quite as localised as the French structure of mayor-led communes, but it was a reasonably close approximation.

One of the benefits of this 'grassroots' approach to local democracy was that the number of residents represented by an individual councillor could be as low as 300–400. Wardle (mentioned above) was a small mill town in a steep-sided valley north of Rochdale, relatively isolated from its neighbouring settlements. The urban district council, its population, at the time of its municipal demise in 1974 was just under 7000. Its functions included (inter alia) housing provision and management, refuse collection, street lighting, certain public health issues and building control (a much wider range of responsibilities than those available to current town and parish councils). Fifteen councillors were elected every four years which meant that each councillor served an average population of 470. Councillors invariably lived within the small wards they represented and would be personally known to many residents, and certainly easily accessible by all. In retrospect, this was an example of place-based local democracy at its best. When it became part of Rochdale MBC in 1974, Wardle ended up with two councillors with a representative load of 3700—eight times higher. The population of Cornwall in 2020 was 572,000 and it had 87 councillors, sitting on a single unitary council for the whole of Cornwall, with each councillor representing 6570 residents, a population per councillor ratio 16 times higher than that in Wardle MBC. Yet this trend has not been seen as a problem by recent governments. By contrast the population of Malta is approximately 444,000 and those citizens are served by 68 municipalities!

A further outcome of the piecemeal but cumulative move to larger authorities is that, over a period of a mere 50 years, towns which were, in 1973, still represented by a local authority have found themselves successively in two increasingly large conglomerate authorities. Take Northwich, a town of real individuality in central Cheshire, whose economic fortunes have been linked to the mining and processing of rock salt. In 1895 it had been established as a municipal borough with a wide range of powers and a population of 20,000. In 1974, it was subsumed within a larger entity comprising a range of small towns, called Vale Royal (population 120,000, whose very name must have been a mystery to many of its residents (everyone knew where Northwich was, but Vale Royal?). Then in 2009, when Vale Royal was abolished, it became part of an even larger authority Chester and Cheshire West with a population of 330,000). This process sits uneasily with recent expressions of enthusiasm for localism which we have heard from central government, as in the 2022 White Paper on Levelling Up.

Before 1974, local government in Wales and Scotland was organised on similar principles to England. In Wales, each individual mining settlement of any size in the southern valleys had its own local authority. In Scotland, the powerful community identity of the small burghs which were scattered throughout the Grampian region (Keith, Elgin, Forres and Lossiemouth) and elsewhere was similarly recognised.

All this has now gone. There were good reasons for the upheaval created by the Local Government Acts of 1963 (covering Greater London) and 1972 and 1973 (covering England and Wales and Scotland respectively), as we acknowledge and explore in the next chapter. But there were viable alternatives to the structures which were introduced, which erased from the government map the likes of Stepney, Bow, Bethnal Green, East Ham, West Ham, Hyde, Dukinfield, Stalybridge and numerous independent towns in Wales and Scotland with equally strong identities. Before 1965, England was not dissimilar to its European comparators in terms of the average size of its local authorities, the closeness of fit between local authorities and community identity and the population per councillor ratio. Since then, there has been a succession of reorganisations, each one of which has increased the average size of councils, increasingly dissociated council boundaries from community identity and progressively increased the population per councillor ratio to a point where there is now a vast difference between where England stands on each of these three measures and the situation in any European country you might care to mention. Our purpose in writing this book is to explain how this alarming outcome has been allowed to occur and suggest what might be done to rectify it.

Why Place Matters

In Deborah Mattinson's insightful 'Beyond the Red Wall' (2020), the importance of the three towns in which her research is conducted—Accrington, Darlington and Stoke-on-Trent—to the people who live there is transparent. Many of them have lived there all their lives and have no intention of moving (or no realistic possibility of doing so). Conservative Party strategists trying to work out how their party can retain control of these parliamentary constituencies at the next election may be well advised to note that in each case, the constituency is represented by a council of the same name (technically, Accrington is part of Hyndburn District council but, in reality, it is by far the largest settlement). They may also do well to note the extent to which the local council features in the lives of residents, who may often be irritated by its actions, but in each case, it was an important reference point and influence on their quality of life.

Place matters. The town where we grew up, the city we chose to move to—indeed all the places we've ever lived—form reference points in our lives bringing with them a potent mix of associations: first girlfriends or boyfriends, where our kids were born, moves to new jobs, and for many of us, the football team we support. Local government expert Barry Quirk (Municipal Journal: November 2017) puts it like this:

> Localities are woven into our personal lives: of where we're from, where we are now, and where we imagine we're going. Specific localities give colour to our origins, our journeys and our imagined destinations. The fabric of locality gives texture to our lives. We may remember with fondness and tenderness the conflicting rhythms of life we experienced in specific places, during specific times in our lives. These memories tether us to places in our past.

What, you may well be wondering, has all this got to do with local government? In our view, it has a great deal. If we have become attached to a place, either because we have always lived there or we have chosen to move there, can we not reasonably expect (or hope) that the place to which we have a commitment is represented by a local council with the power to safeguard and improve its social, economic and environmental well-being? Twenty years ago, the report of the Lyons Enquiry into local government (Lyons, 2007) coined the phrase 'place shaping' to characterise the importance of local authorities taking a strategic, proactive view of the future of the locality, in a way which includes but also transcends their responsibilities for service provision. But as we saw in Chap. 1, 'place-shaping', an admirable objective, only really makes sense if applied to real places with which local people identify, rather than meaningless conglomerate authorities, created on the basis of the misconception that 'bigger is better'. Take the example of Cheshire East, which was established in 2009, as part of the damaging and unnecessary reorganisation initiative of 2006–08 (see Chisholm & Leach, 2008). Cheshire East, a meaningless conglomerate if ever there was one, replaced three councils which reflected and represented 'real places': Macclesfield, Congleton and Crewe (and Nantwich). The result has been that in such authorities 'place shaping' has become a process by which the authorities concerned seek to imbue the artificial areas they cover with some level of public identity and loyalty: a pointless exercise, particularly when it is recognised we already have in England legions of real places, shaped by centuries of lived experience and local loyalties.

We can see how such local loyalties operate in considering the relationship between place and football. It is apparent that, for many, supporting a football team is a potent expression of attachment to place (see Leach, 2020:1–10). In the 2017–18 season, Macclesfield Town, to the delight of their supporters, won promotion from the National League to the Football League, despite having one of the smallest budgets in the League. Did Cheshire East put on a celebratory event to mark the team's achievement? It did not. Why—because expressions of sub-council loyalty have to be expunged if a council with artificial boundaries and containing a conglomerate of areas, is to be made to seem 'real'. Had there still been a Macclesfield-based council, we suspect the outcome would have been different.

The significance which real places have in the lives of local people is well illustrated by the role of football clubs. At their best, they can operate as a source of local pride in the local town or city in which they are located and a potent symbol of the strength of personal attachment to these places. When Walsall, or Carlisle United or Cheltenham Town play at Wembley, in a cup final or play-off decider, the town's inhabitants typically turn out in force, even when they otherwise rarely watch the team. This is the day when the achievements and indeed the very existence of these places are brought to the attention of a wider public; an occasion for celebrating attachment to a place which has a genuine community identity and a profound significance in the residents' lives. And, in the three examples mentioned, there exists a local authority with a mandate to seek to improve the quality of life of the town's inhabitants and to be praised or complained about in so far as their efforts succeed or fail. But this scenario would not have quite the same resonance, would it, if the towns concerned were within Cheshire East or North Northamptonshire?

Our worry is that, as the move to large unitary authorities continues, so the balance between local authorities which represent real places and those which do not becomes tilted increasingly toward the latter. Take, for example, the recently established unitary authority of North Northamptonshire. As we discuss in Chap. 5 its origins were bizarre. In 2016, Northamptonshire County Council was in severe financial difficulties—by no means the first council to experience this problem since 1983. The remedy recommended by the nominated inspector and imposed by the government was for the county and generally well-performing districts to be abolished, and two new unitary authorities—North and West Northamptonshire respectively—to be established to replace them.

As a result of this ad hoc and illogical reorganisation, four authorities representing real places have now disappeared from the local government map and been replaced by a meaningless conglomerate that it is hard to imagine anyone ever identifying with. Corby, Kettering and Wellingborough were all authorities which comprised a sizeable central town within a rural catchment area. Even East Northants, the fourth district to be condemned, was focused on a group of adjacent small towns (Rushden, Irthlingborough and Higham Ferres), specialising in the manufacture of boots and shoes and with their own football team (the colourfully-named Rushden and Diamonds FC.) The district had a raison d'etre and a distinctive identity, as was even more the case with Corby, Kettering and Wellingborough. The same cannot be said for North Northamptonshire nor for others of its ilk, such as Central Bedfordshire, which can only be described as 'non-places'.

A healthy democracy is one in which there are a range of incentives for local people to participate in the political life of the area in which they live. These opportunities are particularly important in a unitary state such as England, where power has become increasingly centralised over the past 40 years or so. This process of local participation has been demonstrated to be more likely to occur if the local authority is one which is congruent with the place with which local people identify (see Chap. 8): Macclesfield, not Cheshire East: Weston-super-Mare not North Somerset.

One of the most worrying effects of the move to large unitary authorities is the reduction in the number of councillors involved in the change (over 60% in North Northamptonshire) and the consequent reduction in the opportunities for local people with political aspirations (including independents) to become councillors. What we see in the process of creating artificial conglomerate councils is a dangerous narrowing of the opportunities for citizens to become involved in local self-government. But, as far as central government is concerned, it would seem that there are advantages in the reduction in the numbers of councillors; it is certainly not a 'problem' which appears to concern them.

Conclusion

In this chapter we have explored why place matters to people and why it should therefore matter to our structure and system of local government. Local loyalties are not something that should be so easily dismissed by those seeking to create large, technocratically shaped and meaningless new entities in a search for the chimera of size-related effective, efficient and economical local government. If local government is to be responsive, locally meaningful and relevant it must reflect the real places where people live. But the direction of journey of English local government has, for some decades now, been away from a notion that local government is about real localities. Rather, it has been about a search for a clinical neatness of structure in local government that, in our view, damagingly undermines local identities and loyalties.

We have seen in this chapter that the centre has a long-term objective for local government towards fewer and fewer units and fewer and fewer councillors. In the next chapter we explore that objective and the process by which the centre is attempting to achieve the de-localisation of local government in England—and why.

References

Brockway, F. (1949). *Bermondsey story: the life of Alfred Salter*. Allen and Unwin.

Chandler, J. A. (2007). *Explaining local government: Local government in Britain since 1800*. Manchester University Press.

Chisholm, M., & Leach, S. (2008). *Botched business: The damaging process of re-organising local government, 2006–2008*. Douglas McLean.

Leach, S. (2020). *Twenty football towns*. Saraband.

Lyons, S. M. (2007). *Place-shaping a shared ambition for the future of local government*. HMSO.

Mattinson, D. (2020). *Beyond the red wall: Why labour lost, how the conservatives won and what will happen next*. Biteback Publishing.

Quirk, B. (2017, November). *Municipal Journal*.

Young, M., & Wilmott, P. (1957). *Family and kinship in East London*. Routledge.

CHAPTER 3

Reorganisation, Reorganisation, Reorganisation: The Changing Map of Local Government

Abstract Central government can take one of two different approaches to local government reorganisation: a system-wide 'root and branch' approach or one focusing on a particular type of authority or part of the country. After 60 years of relative structural stability, two royal commissions were established, the Herbert Commission (which reported in 1961) which dealt with the Greater London metropolis and the Redcliffe-Maud Commission (which reported in 1969) which covered the rest of England. Both were tasked with recommending a structure which took into account the large increase in journey-to-work traffic particularly in and around Greater London and the major provincial city regions. In each case a two-tier county-district system was the eventual outcome, but with districts composed of amalgamations of existing urban and rural authorities, which severed the link between community identity and local authority definition. Subsequent reorganisations (the abolition of GLC and the metropolitan counties (1986), the Banham Commission (1995) and the Labour government's 2006–08 initiative), all partial reorganisations, have continued the move to larger local authorities, with the introduction of unitary (all-purpose) authorities becoming increasingly common.

Keywords Local government reorganisation • Local government size • Devolution • London Government • County councils • District

S. Leach, C. Copus, *The Strange Demise of the Local in Local Government*, Palgrave Studies in Sub-National Governance, https://doi.org/10.1007/978-3-031-32819-0_3

councils • Levelling up • Regions • Relationship between authority size and cost-effectiveness • Unitary authorities • Two-tier local government

Introduction

One of the key features of local government in England, and the rest of the UK, is the relative ease with which the centre (including the governments of Scotland and Wales) can reorganise and restructure the entire system of local government, or parts of it. No special constitutional process is required. While commissions and inquires may be held—an approach which has rapidly declined since the 1990s—and while consultation and negotiation will be undertaken between the centre and local government—the power to change the shape, size and boundaries of units of local government is a one which rests wholly with the centre.

Government can take two main approaches to reorganisation: a system-wide, root-and-branch approach, which redraws the entire map of local government and touches, in some way, every existing council: or, a more limited approach which focuses on types of councils, geographical areas or simply sees and seizes an opportunity for local government reorganisation wherever it occurs. In this chapter we examine how these two approaches have been employed over the past 60 years, and the implications and outcomes for local government. We explore the commissions and inquiries that have been held into local government structure, and the more ad hoc initiatives in each case exploring the different political objectives and assumptions involved.

The next section of the chapter examines what happened to London Government, following the Herbert commission's report of 1961. Section three examines how the local government map of England was torn apart and reassembled following the Redcliffe-Maud commission's report of 1969. Subsequent sections deal with the various piecemeal reorganisations proposed or carried out between 1979 and 2022. The chapter concludes by drawing together the lessons that can be learned from the centre's approach to local government reorganisation.

You Have to Start Somewhere: London

After over 60 years of relative stability across local government, London was the focus for the first of a series of local government reorganisations and upheavals which have been regularly instigated ever since. In 1961 the Conservative Government established a Royal Commission, chaired by Sir George Herbert, to make recommendations as to how London should be governed, at a time of rapidly increasing traffic growth and when the journey-to-work catchment area of the metropolis had expanded greatly since the London County Council was formed in 1888. The government of London had always posed the centre with a complex question about the recognition of the special place of London in sub-national government, alongside the need to constrain its political and economic muscle (see Jackson, 1965; Rhodes, 1970; Owen, 1982; Saint, 1989; Travers, 2004). The 1960s proved a tipping point for how the centre started to assess the structural patterns of local government, one which has had consequences for the future of local government across the country ever since.

There are two principal criteria on which a major reorganisation of local government of the type that occurred in London in 1965 can be justified. First, the 'fitness for purpose' argument that changes in the socio-economic patterns of living, working, transport and recreation mean that the existing governmental arrangements are no longer congruent with the new patterns which have emerged. Second, the economies of scale argument—that a system based on larger authorities than those currently in existence would be more efficient and cost-effective in its capacity to provide local services. The first of these criteria provides a stronger justification than the latter, where attempts to demonstrate a relationship between size and enhanced cost-effectiveness have always been contentious and contested (Dollery & Crase, 2004; Lassen & Serretzlew, 2011). There has always been a challenge of reconciling the implications of applying this criterion with the case for retaining a pattern of local government which bears some resemblance to the places and communities with which people identify and have a degree of affinity and loyalty—for example, Huddersfield rather than Kirklees, Ashton-under-Lyne rather than Tameside, Halifax rather than Calderdale.

The primary justification for the Herbert Commission review of London Government was that of 'fitness for purpose'. In the 1950s and early 1960s, it had become apparent that in London, the combined impact of population growth and changing transportation pressures (principally resulting from the increased use of the motor car) had resulted in the fact that London County Council (LCC) no longer remotely approximated to the journey-to-work catchment area of Greater London. In effect, by this point, the LCC represented 'inner London', but excluded places like Wimbledon, Ilford, Barnet and Richmond which were widely seen as part of the great metropolis. A new authority covering the reality of London's expansion, and capable of dealing with complex interconnections between land-use, roads and public and private transport was required, or so it was argued. The establishment of a Greater London Council (GLC), which covered the wide area that now was seen to constitute 'London' as a sub-region was indeed what the Herbert Commission recommended.

The case for the GLC replacing the LCC was, at the time, widely accepted, but there was a further, more controversial challenge facing the Commission, namely, what to do with the local government structures which existed within the area of the LCC, and in the areas outside the LCC which were to be incorporated into its boundaries. In Inner London, as noted in Chap. 2, there existed a pattern of local government which typically reflected its 'urban villages'—places like Hampstead, Bethnal Green, Bermondsey and Chelsea, with names familiar to residents and tourists alike, and which embodied a link between local community and local authority. There were 28 of these boroughs, with populations typically around 80,000. In the outer area incorporated into the GLC, there were sizeable portions of the counties of Essex, Kent and Surrey and the whole of Middlesex (abolished as a consequence of the reorganisation), together with a mixture of large county boroughs such as Croydon, Bromley, East Ham and West Ham and a host of smaller urban and rural districts and municipal boroughs, most of them based on places with strong community identities.

The Herbert Commission decided that a system which perpetuated the existing inner London Boroughs and all or most of the lower-tier councils in outer London was not sustainable. It opted for a superficially neat pattern of consolidation into larger units, proposing 32 London Boroughs within the newly defined GLC area, with populations ranging between 200,000 and 150,000. But the Commission did accept that a two-tier system of the GLC and London Boroughs was the right solution, even if the size of the second tier was increased considerably.

In inner London, the process of amalgamation involved between 2 and 3 existing boroughs, resulting in 12 new London Boroughs. Thus Camberwell, Southwark and Peckham became the new Southwark. In the process many familiar place names (Hampstead, Stepney, Bethnal Green and Brixton) disappeared from the local government map and some unfamiliar newcomers—Tower Hamlets, Merton and Brent—took their place. In outer London, a similar process of amalgamation was recommended where the 54 extant local authorities were replaced by 20 new London Boroughs. Tourists must have struggled to identify the locations of Havering, Redbridge and Brent, as much as their residents had problems identifying with them. Indeed, when the Essex county boroughs of East Ham and West Ham were merged along with North Woolwich (part of the metropolitan borough of Woolwich, which crossed the river Thames) finding a suitable name was equally a problem. Naming new councils is always a contentious process and in the latter case the rather sterile name of 'Newham' was created (see Travers, 2015). While the name has no local roots, the word Ham or Hamme is found in an Anglo-Saxon charter of 958 and a subsequent charter of 1037, which relates to that area. It would be nice to think those responsible for the name of the new borough had this in mind when the appellation 'New' was attached to Ham, rather than just keeping the 'Ham' from East and West as a matter of convenience.

It is in the examples above where we see how the reorganisation of London Government in 1965 made two important breaks with tradition and set future precedents, which had major implications for later reorganisations. First it broke the link, in the Greater London area, between community identity and local authorities; the first time this had happened since the various local government reorganisations of the late nineteenth century. Had the authorities which disappeared from the map enjoyed the same constitutional status as the French communes, this change would have been much more difficult, if not impossible, to implement. But they did not, and despite protests from many of the established councils affected, the Commission's proposals became law in the London Government Act 1963—with the new councils starting life in 1965.

Secondly, the changes involved the introduction of the 'bigger is better' narrative and justification for change, which has continued to the present day, in what has proved to be a long period of structural upheaval. Larger councils would be better equipped to provide efficient and effective services than smaller ones, or so the narrative assumes. The assumptions underpinning 'bigger is better', the validity of which has never been convincingly justified, have become an increasingly dominant feature of the subsequent discourse about structural change (this justification was, however, conveniently ignored, when the GLC was abolished by the Thatcher government in 1986). The Herbert Commission identified the need for a strategic authority which encompassed the whole of Greater London. But even though it promoted a two-tier London, in its proposals at a sub-GLC level, it broke the link between community identity and councils and introduced an economies of scale criterion into the debate which, then and since, has proved controversial and unhelpful.

Carving Up the Local Government Map of the Rest of England

The problems faced in the metropolis in the 1960s in dealing with population growth and the spectacular rise in the use of the motor car (particularly in relation to journeys to work) were also affecting the provincial metropolitan areas, including Greater Manchester, Merseyside, the West Midlands, West Yorkshire, and Tyne and Wear. In Greater Manchester, there was a complex advisory network organisation known as SELNEC (south-east Lancashire and north-east Cheshire) charged with producing a land-use transportation strategy for the whole area and struggling to do so, given the wide range of conflicting local interests involved.

The government's response was to establish in 1966 a second Royal Commission, chaired by Lord Redcliffe-Maud. In those days, that was what governments did when faced with complex problems of this nature; appoint a panel of experts and allow them two or three years to assemble evidence and make recommendations. This process had a lot to recommend it, although it has rarely been used since the 1970s. It had the effect of dissociating the process of analysis and the development of proposals from party-political considerations (although it must be said, governments did not always accept or implement the recommendations of such bodies). From the 1970s onwards, party politics has played an increasing role in the local government reorganisations, often to the detriment of analytical rigour and the viability of the proposals.

The Redcliffe-Maud report, which covered England and Wales, followed the example of the Herbert Commission in proposing the establishment of metropolitan counties, with responsibilities which were similar to those allocated to the GLC, in Greater Manchester, Merseyside and the West Midlands (though not elsewhere). Within these areas, lower-tier authorities similar in population size and with similar functions to those of the London boroughs were recommended. It was in the resulting search for names for these new councils which were acceptable to all (or most) of the dominant predecessor authorities that the likes of Sefton, Tameside, Sandwell and Trafford were conceived.

The creation of the metropolitan counties was a response to the socio-economic and journey pattern changes in these areas (although the cities of Manchester, Liverpool and Birmingham were far from happy with what they perceived to be their reduced status). More controversially, the Redcliffe-Maud Commission had bought into the 'bigger is better' assumption of its predecessor (see Wood, 1976). As a result, it was goodbye to Ashton-under-Lyne, Hyde, Dukinfield, Stalybridge and all the rest, and welcome to Tameside: a further nail in the coffin of local authorities based on communities of real significance to local people. But even more controversial were the Commission's proposals for local government in the non-metropolitan areas of England. The long-established two-tier system of government involving counties within which were a range of lower-tier authorities with a wide range of different shapes and sizes (1250 of them in total) was to be swept away and replaced by a mere 58 unitary (or all-purpose) authorities with an average size in excess of 500,000 (today that would be an average size of around 965,000). Had it been implemented, this proposal, together with the changes recommended in the metropolitan areas, would have resulted in the number of councillors in England being reduced by 85%, an outcome with serious detrimental implications for the democratic viability of the local state.

The Redcliffe-Maud commission accepted the developing 'Bigger is Better' narrative, meaning that councils should cover areas sufficiently expansive to provide efficient services and ensure effective use of resources. Again however, the evidence to support this notion was contested and Wood (1976) suggests the estimates of population size needed were produced by local government professionals to suit what they perceived to be the specifics of their own services.

The commission made the following point about population size:

> There can be no firm rule about the maximum size of an authority. But we concluded that the range of population, from about 250,000 to not much above 1,000,000, which we considered most suitable on functional and organisational grounds for authorities administering all local government services, was also appropriate on democratic grounds (1969 para: 276, p.73).

The commission went on to say, in a comment that introduced the ahistorical term 'unitary' into the lexicon of local government:

> Wherever we could find coherent areas which made good units for planning and transportation and also contained a population of about 250,000 to about 1,000,000, we would combine responsibility for all services in a single authority for each area. We call such areas unitary and the authorities responsible for them unitary authorities (para 277:73)

But the Commission baulked at creating councils that were too large and recognising the diseconomies of scale that could occur, and the solution would be to operate a two-tier system *(para278:73)*. Indeed, the final report of the commission is a continual struggle to justify the need for larger councils, but at the same time reconcile the damage done to local representation and public attachment to local government by making councils too large (HMSO, 1969); for example, the commission noted that: *Moreover, the bigger the unit, the more doubtful it becomes whether the individual citizen can have a real sense of belonging to it* (para: 275, 1969) but throughout accepted the evidence of local government professionals that councils needed to increase their size considerably.

Although public protests about issues specific to a particular local authority have been and remain commonplace, it is rare for an issue to transcend the local and expand into a nationwide campaign. But the '58 unitary authority' proposal of the Redcliffe-Maud Commission and its acceptance in 1970 by the then Labour government, based on a calculation that Labour would dominate that structure of local government, triggered one such campaign. Across the shire counties of England and Wales, people began to make their concerns felt, under the banner of the imaginative strapline 'Don't vote for R. E. Mote!'. It is unlikely that the Labour government would have scrapped the proposal; but this question became academic when the Conservatives won the 1970 general election, before the Commission's proposals had been implemented.

The Conservatives proved more responsive. Recognising that their support was strongest in the shire counties, they rejected the move to large unitary authorities and retained most of the existing counties and the two-tier system which operated within them. However, they did follow the commitment to amalgamation which the Commission had recommended for the districts in three provincial metropolitan areas (to which the Conservative government added West Yorkshire, South Yorkshire and Tyne and Wear). The existing mix of county boroughs, municipal boroughs and urban and rural districts in what came to be known as the shire counties were consolidated into shire districts with an average population of around 120,000. At this scale, many familiar cities and large-and medium-sized towns survived (Cambridge, Durham, Mansfield, Chester) often with extended boundaries drawing in rural hinterlands. But in many cases the process of amalgamation resulted in arbitrary combinations, which (as with the London Boroughs and metropolitan districts) struggled to reach agreement on acceptable names for the new entities. Copus et al. (2017: 102–107) have categorised the confected names for new councils that arose as part of the amalgamation process as: compass point councils, 'ampersand' councils and 'non-existent places councils—with the later normally, but not exclusively, deriving a name from some topographical feature.

As a result, we have authorities such as: North Kesteven, South Cambridgeshire and East Hertfordshire, North-West Leicestershire; Oadby and Wigston, Newark and Sherwood, Crewe and Nantwich; Waverley (named after Waverley Abbey), Hyndburn (named after a river), Hambleton (named after Hambleton Hills, part of the North York Moors), the Vale of White Horse Council (named after a Valley with a pre-historic carving of a white horse) and Three Rivers council (named, not surprisingly, after three local rivers: the Chess, the Gade and the Colne). All these council names would be likely to prove confusing to residents and visitors alike and are indicative of the breaking of the link between local community identity and the local council which has become commonplace across England.

The deleterious impact on local democracy of overall impact of the changes incorporated in the 1972 Local Government Act was seen in the brutal reduction in the total number of local authorities in England by two-thirds (from 1210 to 412) and in Wales from 184 to 45. The long-term link between the towns and area with which people identified and local government units had been largely destroyed.

A separate Royal Commission was established in Scotland (the Wheatley Commission) which reported in 1973. It recommenced a similar outcome to that which was eventually adopted in England and Wales: a two-tier system across the mainland with nine regional authorities (including Strathclyde, with a population of 2.5 million) and 53 district councils (including Glasgow and Edinburgh), plus all-purpose authorities for the Orkneys, the Shetlands and the Western Isles. The net effect was a reduction in the number of councils from 431 to 65.

Over a period of a mere ten years (1965–74) the local government map of Great Britain had been transformed. What had started out as a response to the need for a strategic land-use transportation planning capacity in Greater London and the major conurbations became a process which ended the existence of the vast majority of local authorities which represented places with real significance for their inhabitants. The managerial perspectives of 'economies of scale', and 'efficient and effective service provision' had confined to history a seventy-year period in which there was a widespread congruence between community identity and the territory covered by local councils.

Further Piecemeal Reorganisations 1979-2000

Given the major investment of time, financial resources and political capital involved in local government reorganisations, there was a widespread expectation that once the new structures were up and running in 1974, they would continue unchanged for the foreseeable future. It was an expectation which proved to be unfounded. The following forty-five years would see a series of further structural interventions, most of them, in one way or another, politically motivated. It is worth stressing again that this kind of arbitrary interference has only proved possible because there are no constitutional safeguards for local government in England of the kind that exist in France, Germany, Switzerland and many other European countries.

The first destabilising political initiative was launched in 1978 by Peter Shore, the Environment Minister in the Labour government who had been returned to power in 1974. He had been lobbied by Labour leaders of the big cities outside the metropolitan county areas, such as Bristol, Nottingham, Derby and Plymouth who were aggrieved that the 1972 Local Government Act had transferred their much-prized responsibilities for education and social services to the shire counties in which they were now situated as district councils. Wishing to placate these cities (usually under Labour control), he issued a white paper entitled 'Organic Change' (a misnomer if ever there was one!) which set out the government's intention of transferring these responsibilities back to the disgruntled cities. The initiative was aborted when Labour lost the 1979 general election and a long period of Conservative government commenced.

But the precedent had been set. If Labour was prepared to tinker around with local government structures so soon after a major reorganisation, for political reasons, what was to stop the Conservatives doing likewise? When the GLC, under the leadership of Ken Livingstone, became increasingly politically strident in the early 1980s, to the extent of attaching banners to the front of County Hall (conveniently situated across the river from the Houses of Parliament) proclaiming the increasingly alarming national unemployment figures, Margaret Thatcher decided to take action. A White Paper (D.o.E, 1983) with the misleading title 'Streamlining the Cities' was issued, which set out proposals to abolish the GLC, with the six metropolitan county councils (all Labour-controlled) thrown in for good measure.

Such a party-political initiative ignored the compelling functional reasons for setting up the GLC and the MCCs in the first place, assumed that the district councils, acting collectively, could equally well perform their strategic functions, using a plethora of joint boards and joint committees with far from transparent accountability mechanisms. It proved an untenable assumption. But the measure was implemented in 1986, despite generating unprecedented levels of public support for Ken Livingstone, previously an easy target for the press.

The expectation of stability, following the implementation of the 1972 reorganisation, was now no longer a plausible position. How long before the next intervention, local government academics and practitioners asked themselves? The answer turned out to be five years! Following the public hostility to the ill-judged introduction of the Poll Tax, and the resulting downfall of Margaret Thatcher in the wake of some disastrous by-election results, it was perceived by the government to be essential to replace the poll tax, with something less divisive. Michael Heseltine was the minister tasked with doing so. In an attempt to avoid the impression of an ignominious political retreat, he set in motion a small-scale departmental review of local government structures, finance and leadership.

The review replaced the poll tax with the council tax, which bore a distinct resemblance to the rates system which the poll tax had been intended to replace. This was the primary purpose of the exercise. Heseltine's own personal enthusiasm for elected mayors also featured in the ensuing report, although there proved to be little support within local government for the idea and it quickly slipped off the agenda, to be revived when Labour came to power in 1997. But the third element was the instigation of yet another review of local government structure in the English shire counties, to be carried out by a Commission chaired by Sir John Banham, a prominent businessman. This option was a welcome move away from the 'political conviction' which had underpinned the abolition of the GLC and the MCCs. But the Banham Commission was left in no doubt about what was expected of it: its terms of reference steered it towards recommendations which would significantly increase the number of unitary authorities in the shires, at the expense of the existing two-tier system of local government. Unitary local government was Heseltine's preference as he has confirmed many times since and especially forcefully in his report for the Government entitled No Stone Unturned (TSO, 2012), and also that of the then Department of the Environment (as has also subsequently become increasingly apparent). It looked as if the Redcliffe-Maud model—large unitary authorities across the whole of non-metropolitan England—was back on the agenda.

To its credit, the Banham Commission, over time, refused to be steered in this direction. After producing a number of draft unitary-based proposals which proved locally controversial, it placed increasing emphasis on research evidence regarding community identity and public opinion, drawing on one of the requirements in its brief—'to reflect the identities and interests of local communities'. The chairman coined the well-judged phrase 'if it ain't broke, don't fix it' to characterise the Commission's change of direction. The eventual outcome, after Sir John had been replaced as chairman by David Cooksey in 1995, was the establishment of 46 new unitary authorities, ranging in size from Rutland (40,000) to Bristol (360,000). This total was far fewer than had originally been anticipated and left large swathes of non-metropolitan England unaffected. Although the Commission had been asked to 'secure effective and convenient local government' which could have been interpreted as a proxy for the familiar 'economies of scale' criterion, it chose to put greater weight on community identity and public opinion, a welcome reintroduction of a consideration which has since come to be increasingly ignored (see Leach (ed) (1998) for a perspective on the Banham Review).

Although the Commission chose not to adopt a major shift in favour of large unitary authorities, it did little to strengthen the link between community identity and council definition (although to be fair, its stance did enable most of those shire districts which still retained this link to survive). Furthermore, it failed to produce a more coherent local government map of England; the overall impact of the implementation of its proposals was to diminish the coherence and consistency of the structure, rather than increase it. A sense of instability and unresolved structural tensions remained.

The fact that local government reorganisation was back on the agenda was exploited in Scotland and Wales by their respective Secretaries of State, who translated John Major's government's enthusiasm for unitary authorities, not by establishing equivalents of the Banham Commission (whose brief was confined to England) but simply by unilaterally introducing proposals of this nature. In Wales, the brief White Paper (HMSO, 1991) claimed that a move to unitary authorities would result in 'greater local identity, greater efficiency and more accountability' (all highly contestable claims). In Scotland, similar assertions were made. By 1994, the local government maps in both countries had been redrawn: in Scotland, the two-tier system was replaced by 29 unitary councils (including three island authorities bringing the total to 32) and in Wales, by 22 unitary authorities. In each country, the number of authorities was reduced by more than half and their average size increased to ten times that of the European average. Particularly notable was the establishment of a single council for the Highlands region—all 9900 square miles of it!

Further Piecemeal Reorganisations: 2000-2022

In the 25 years since the Banham/Cooksey Commissions completed their work the reorganisation bandwagon has rolled on, re-emerging every few years in different forms, but with a similar focus—a move to creating more unitary authorities in increasing numbers of two-tier county council areas.

The 1997–2001 Labour government quickly acknowledged the strength of the case for the reintroduction of a democratically elected unit of local government to cover the whole of Greater London and established the Greater London Authority (GLA) (including an elected mayor for London) which commenced operation in 2000. In 2006, a strange new variant into the sequence of reorganisation initiatives was introduced. The White Paper 'Strong and Prosperous Communities' included a provision encouraging local authorities in the shire counties (whether counties or districts) to submit bids to become unitary authorities. There was no apparent political incentive for such an initiative; 'civil service pressure on a new minister' provides a more likely explanation (see Chap. 4). The resulting process was summarised by Michael Chisholm and Steve Leach (2008, p. 152) in the following terms:

> Unreliable data was accepted by the Department, inconsistent decisions were taken and misleading information given as a basis for those decisions. Parliament was misled and there was a large element of political deception

The eventual outcome of this cack-handed process was that ten additional unitary authorities were established, most of them county-based, with relatively large populations (on average, 300–400,000). As a result, many real places disappeared from the local government map, including Durham City, Shrewsbury, Macclesfield, Crewe, Chester (although its name survived in Cheshire West and Chester) and all the individual distinctive towns in Cornwall. All were swallowed up in large unitary counties or semi-counties.

There was a welcome hiatus between 2010 and 2014 when Eric Pickles, the minister responsible for local government in the Conservative/Liberal Democrat coalition, made it clear that he regarded reorganisation as a distraction from the bigger issues in his department (notably the impact of austerity). Towards the end of this administration in 2014, the Chancellor George Osborne announced that he had agreed a devolution deal with the Greater Manchester Combined Authority (which is comprised of the leaders of the ten authorities which cover the area of the former Greater Manchester Metropolitan County Council), in what became known as the 'Northern Powerhouse' initiative. A condition was attached to the deal that the authorities concerned had to agree to the direct election of a Greater Manchester mayor. This requirement in effect reintroduced a two-tier system of local government in the city region. This initiative was soon extended to Merseyside, South Yorkshire and the West Midlands and later elsewhere (the West of England, the Tees Valley, South Tyneside and (perhaps more surprisingly) Cornwall and Peterborough and Cambridgeshire). It was in effect yet another local government reorganisation, but one that was Treasury-inspired and administered, rather than something that was owned by the Department of Communities, Housing and Local Government (DCHLG), the department then responsible for the oversight of local government. It had no implications for the Department's 'large unitary authority' agenda—or so it appeared.

But in February 2016, as the Cities and Local Government Bill, the legislative basis of the burgeoning devolution initiative, was being discussed in the House of Lords, a strange twist to its scope was introduced. There were now to be two bidding processes which could result in groups of local authorities being awarded devolved powers and resources by the government. The first was the already established route—a deal with a directly-elected mayor (although Cornwall appeared to have been granted an exception to this condition). The second required an agreement on the part of the authorities concerned to move from the existing two-tier arrangements to a unitary system, a pathway which did not require an elected mayor. What had started out as a relatively circumscribed 'Northern Powerhouse' initiative had been transformed into yet another move on the part of the Department to introduce more unitary authorities (see Leach et al., 2018, pp 145–6 for further details).

Much frenetic activity ensued. At first, there was a requirement that there should be consensus amongst the county and district authorities concerned as to the preferred unitary structure. This outcome was always unlikely and respective proposals in Kent, Oxfordshire and Northants (amongst others) failed to overcome this hurdle. But over time, the 'consensus' requirement was quietly (very quietly!) dropped, and new county-based unitary authorities were given the go-ahead in Buckinghamshire and Dorset (where Christchurch was hived off, much against its will, to a new unitary authority amalgamating Bournemouth and Poole).

Without doubt, the most bizarre addition to this list occurred in 2018, when Northamptonshire County Council (the large upper tier authority) was identified as a failing authority (indeed one unlikely to be able to set a legal budget) following a Best Value inspection. The government's inspector's report recommended a structural change, replacing the existing two-tier system with two unitary authorities—North and West Northamptonshire, both with populations between 300,000 and 400,000. The justification for this recommendation is strange indeed. The report argued that the problems faced by the County Council are now so deep and ingrained that it is not possible to promote a recovery plan which could bring the council back to stability and safety in a reasonable time-scale (DCHLGC, 2018, p 36). It added that 'to change the culture and organisational ethos and restore balance would take of the order of five years and require a substantial cash injection' (ibid. p37). It concluded that 'a way forward with a clean sheet' was required, in their view the two unitary authority 'solution' noted above. However, if larger councils are always perceived to be better, it was perhaps inconsistent on the part of DCHLG that the larger, top-tier county council was to be abolished; in this case, it appears that bigger was not better! It was the lower-tier districts councils who in most cases were performing well, that came to be abolished as a consequence of the upper tier council's failure (see Chap. 5 for further details of this bizarre process).

When 'failing authorities' had been identified in the early 2000s (Walsall and Hackney were two such examples, and subsequently Tower Hamlets 2013), the government's response had been to appoint a team of interventionist commissioners to identify and impose measures for sorting out the problems concerned, which they invariably succeeded in doing within a year or so (rather than the five years forecast in inspector's report!). That would seem to have been the most appropriate response in Northamptonshire. The idea of responding to a financial crisis by abolishing the council concerned sets a worrying precedent. Liverpool City Council is, at the time of writing, undergoing a similar financial crisis. Will the government's response be to replace the City Council with two new authorities—North Liverpool and South Liverpool? And watch out Newcastle, Birmingham and Sheffield, it could be your turn next!

In November 2019, a Conservative government with a large majority was elected, mainly due to a switch of voter preference in what came to be known as the 'red wall' constituencies (places like Bishop Auckland, Workington, Bolsover and Grimsby). The prime minister, Boris Johnson, no doubt grateful for this unexpected source of support, soon announced an initiative designated as 'levelling up', a term which implies a process of economic regeneration in such places which would bring them up to the levels of prosperity enjoyed in other parts of the country. The concept was thin on detail and (in 2023) remains so. However, its first tangible manifestation appeared within the DCHLG and, true to form, it included a further move in the direction of large unitary authorities. The DCHLG package embraced commitments to spreading devolution to more local authorities, to continue the momentum established in the Northern Powerhouse policy and to developing structures which would facilitate economic regeneration in the aftermath of the Covid pandemic and would thus contribute to the government's 'levelling up' agenda. The introduction of large unitary authorities to replace what the government perceived to be the 'out-dated' two-tier system which still operated in the shire counties was highlighted as a means of achieving these objectives. The Levelling-Up white paper (TSO, 2022:318) refers to the arena of local government as one of: '*fragmentation and administrative complexity*' and spuriously links economic growth to the need for unitary local government. Yet again, the unitary principle had found its way into an area of government policy where it was by no means apparent that it belonged.

Conclusion

The structure, shape and size of local government units have, over the decades, become subject to frequent alteration by the centre, either to implement its own policies on local government or to implement various government policy priorities that are operationalised by and through local government. A dual pressure on the size of local authorities has thus been exerted. But following the comprehensive reorganisations of London Government in the mid-1960s and the subsequent reorganisation of the rest of the Great Britain in the early 1970s, further reorganisations have been piecemeal and opportunistic in nature. No sign of a further 'root and branch' initiative has emerged.

There has been a comprehensive embracing of the 'bigger is better' narrative at the centre when it comes to the shape and size of local government. That embracing is based however on political/administrative objectives, rather than any clear assessment of what independent, international research has to say about local government size (which we review in Chap. 8). It is what is convenient to the centre that is driving local government reorganisation in England.

What we have seen in England since the two major reorganisations is a disjointed series of opportunistic attempts by the centre to move towards the sort of structure set out by Maud in 1969—large-scale unitary councils across the whole of England. The uneven progress of this policy initiative, which can helpfully be characterised as 'reorganisation by stealth' is examined in more detail in Chap. 6, where its worrying implications for the future of local government are highlighted. But first it is important to seek to explain the long-term dominance of the large unitary authority model in the departmental culture of DLUHC and its predecessors.

References

Chisholm, M., & Leach, S. (2008). *Botched business: The damaging process of re-organising local government, 2006–2008.* Douglas McLean.

Copus, C., Roberts, M., & Wall, R. (2017). *Local government in England: Centralisation, autonomy and control.* Palgrave Macmillan.

DCHLG. (2018). *Best value report on Northamptonshire County Council.*

Department of the Environment. (D.o.E). (1983). *Streamlining the cities: Government proposals for reorganising local government in Greater London and the Metropolitan counties.* Department of the Environment.

Dollery, B., & Crase, L. (2004). *Is bigger local government better? An evaluation of the economic case for Australian Municipal amalgamation programs.* Working Paper Series in Economics No. 2004-4.

HMSO. (1969). Royal Commission on Local Government, Vol. 1 Report, cm 4040 (Redcliffe-Maud).

HMSO. (1991). *Local government in Wales; A charter for the future.*

Jackson, W. E. (1965). *Achievement: A short history of the LCC.* Longmans.

Lassen, D., & Serretzlew, S. (2011). Jurisdiction size and local democracy: Evidence on internal political efficacy from large-scale municipal reform. *American Political Science Review, 105*(2), 238–258.

Leach, S. (1998). The local government review: A policy perspective. In S. Leach (Ed.), *Local government reorganisation: The review and its aftermath.* Frank Cass.

Leach, S., Stewart, J., & Jones, G. (2018). *Centralisation, devolution and the future of local government in England.* Routledge.

Owen, D. (1982). *The government of Victorian London 1855–1889: The Metropolitan board of works, the vestries and the city corporation.* Harvard University Press.

Rhodes, G. (1970). *The government of London: The struggle for reform.* Weidenfeld and Nicolson.

Royal Commission on Local Government, Vol. 1 Report, cm 4040, 1969 (Redcliffe-Maud).

Saint, A. (1989). *Politics and the people of London: The London County Council 1889–1965.* Hambledon Press.

Travers, T. (2004). *The politics of London, governing an ungovernable city.* Palgrave Macmillan.

Travers, T. (2015). *London's boroughs at 50.* Biteback Publishing.

TSO. (2012). Heseltine, M, *No stone unturned in pursuit of growth.*

TSO. (2022). Levelling Up the United Kingdom CP604.

Wood, B. (1976). *The process of local government reform 1966-74.* George Allen and Unwin.

CHAPTER 4

Explaining the Persistence of the Unitary Principle in the Department's Mindset

Abstract Since the Banham Commission reported in 1995, there have been a number of opportunistic attempts by successive Labour and Conservative governments to establish large (300,000 population and above) unitary authorities in shire counties operating a two-tier system. Such initiatives have often been announced by newly appointed ministers with little previous experience of or interest in local government issues. The question is raised as to whether this phenomenon can best be explained in terms of 'departmental policy': something which is presented to new ministers as 'good practice', despite the lack of evidence that large unitary authorities achieve the claims made for them. Evidence from the 2006–08 'bidding process' and from the recent reorganisation in Cumbria supports a hypothesis that this is indeed the most plausible explanation of events.

Keywords Unitary councils • Local government size • Two-tier local government • Local democracy • Levelling up • Reorganisation • Combined authority • Subsidiarity • Councillors • Economic regeneration

S. Leach, C. Copus, *The Strange Demise of the Local in Local Government*, Palgrave Studies in Sub-National Governance,
https://doi.org/10.1007/978-3-031-32819-0_4

Introduction

We noted in the last chapter that since the inception of county boroughs, single-tier local government has been an established feature of the local government landscape. What has changed is the extent to which the unitary principle is being applied in local government reorganisations. We also pointed out that the Redcliffe-Maud report, published in 1969, introduced the term 'unitary' into the terminology of local government. Over the 50 years since the publication of that report, the unitary authority principle has become ever more firmly established in the assumptive world of DLUHC and its various predecessors, embodying an unsubstantiated (and rarely justified) view that unitary local government is the ideal model for local authorities. In this chapter we examine how this has come to be the case.

Government departments, faced with periodic changes in governments and more frequent changes in ministers and ministerial teams, typically develop their own policy preferences (e.g. the Foreign Office was widely perceived to be 'pro Europe' in the run up to the 2015 EU referendum). All government departments are, of course, required to take on board the policy agenda of an incoming administration and minister and to find ways of implementing it (or persuading ministers that their priorities are unachievable, or only so in a modified form). But in relatively low-profile departments, such as the Department of Levelling-Up Housing and Communities (DLUHC) (which has gone through numerous name changes since the 1960s, but whose portfolio has always included local government) there may not be many 'big policy issues' to which incoming ministers are committed. In these circumstances, they may be receptive to suggestions from senior civil servants about initiatives they might take (or reintroduce) which would raise their profile and enhance their ministerial career prospects.

In the chapter we address the following question: how is it that a succession of ministers, in both Labour and Conservative administrations, have been prepared to take it up and argue for unitary local government? In the next section we explore the reasons why the unitary principle is so ingrained in the centre's thinking. Section 3 sets out the opportunistic approach that the centre has taken to seize chances to merge councils and create new unitary authorities. The conclusion provides a brief overview of the arguments in the chapter.

The Unitary Bandwagon Develops Momentum 2000–10

Our hypothesis is that local government reorganisation is an example of a policy initiative which owes more to tacit deep-rooted departmental policy preferences than it does to explicit political objectives. As we have seen, after the Banham, and later Cooksey, Commissions and the 1992 Local Government Act, which allowed the Secretary of State to create new unitary councils, there was a lull in the unitary momentum. But, it reappeared on the agenda in 2005, during the Labour government's third term of office in the form of a bizarre 'bidding system' for reorganisation proposals. It then disappeared during the term of office of Eric Pickles (2010–15) who made it clear that he regarded it as a distraction at a time of austerity. But it then re-emerged towards the end of the 2010–15 Conservative administration as an adjunct to George Osborne' Northern powerhouse initiative and stuttered along in a piecemeal fashion during Theresa May's time as prime minister. It was repackaged in 2020, at an early stage of the Johnson-led Conservative administration, as a potential contribution to the 'levelling up' agenda and predicated on an economic regeneration objective. But despite its frequent reappearances, at no time over the past 25 years can it be regarded as an issue of high or even moderate political salience. Local government reorganisation *per se* hardly ever is, which is not surprising, as it is hard to see it as a vote winner.

By far the most convincing explanation of the persistence of a reorganisation agenda, premised on a preference for large unitary authorities, lies in a departmental enthusiasm for this option, which can be brought to the attention of ministers whose own agendas or those of their parties do not preclude it even if it is not seen as a priority. When David Miliband became Secretary of State at the Department of Communities Housing and Local Government (DCHLG) in 2005, he set in motion a stream of work that focused on neighbourhood empowerment and (with prompting from civil servants?) a return to the reorganisation agenda, with authorities across the shire counties of England being asked to develop proposals for unitary local government in their areas, or for an improved version of two-tier working. This initiative appeared to be premised on a belief, unconfirmed by evidence, that there was a major problem with the two-tier system of local government in the shire counties. However, it was not long before he was moved to the position of Foreign Secretary in 2006, and succeeded by a series of ministers—Ruth Kelly, Hazel Blears and John Healey—two of whom came to the job with little if any experience of or apparent interest in local government (the exception being Hazel Blears who had been a Salford City councillor before being elected as an MP).

It was during the period of high ministerial turnover, after David Miliband became Foreign Secretary, that the Department was able to persuade the ministers concerned to embark on a further reorganisation initiative. This bizarre process, which was characterised in effect by competitive bidding, was launched in October 2006. Frequent ministerial turnover provides an ideal opportunity for 'helpful briefings' from civil servants which include their own policy preferences. In this case, there are potential advantages for incoming ministers in being associated with something as tangible as a reorganisation.

Individual local authorities (or groups of them) within counties were invited, by the department, to submit bids to move from the existing two-tier system to some form of unitary alternative. Five criteria were set out:

- Proposals must be affordable
- supported by a broad cross-section of partners and stakeholders
- provide strong, effective and accountable strategic leadership
- deliver genuine opportunities for neighbourhood flexibility and empowerment
- deliver value for money and equity on public services
- (DCLG, 2006)

Twenty-six such bids were received from local authorities at the end of the three-month period earmarked for submissions, a period of such brevity that the capacity of councils to draw up coherent, well-argued, evidence-based bids was greatly constrained and compromised. Of these proposals, 10 were eliminated in March 2007 with 16 proceeding to stakeholder consultation. Of these, a further nine were rejected in July 2007 (or a few months later, following further financial assessments). In December 2007 (and in one case—Bedfordshire—March 2008) it was announced that seven proposals involving a total of nine new unitary authorities would be implemented.

In 'Botched Business', Chisholm and Leach's detailed analysis of the 2006–08 reorganisation process, the authors identify four criteria which can justifiably be applied in the evaluation of an exercise of this level of constitutional importance (2008:7):

- The objectives are clear and consistent with other relevant central government objectives.
- The 'rules of the game' are clarified at the outset and applied consistently throughout the process.
- Proposals are developed on the basis of a thorough review of the available evidence and using an appropriate methodology.
- The justification for a set of proposals is clear and consistent.

Regrettably, the authors conclude, not one of these criteria was met (Chisholm & Leach, 2008:148–9). The rules were not met because they were changed as the process progressed, in particular with regard to the interpretation of the five criteria set out by DCLG. For example, whereas in the initial formulation, it was stated that any proposal must conform to the five criteria, this was later diluted to a 'reasonable expectation' (ibid., p.23) that the criteria would be met, once a new council had been established. Although 'service users and citizens' were initially recognised as having an interest, public opinion was discounted or ignored when citizens were opposed to proposals.

Inconsistency was rife in the way in which evidence was evaluated and the five criteria applied. The DCLG decision letters reveal a selective use of evidence, misleading presentations of evidence and a reliance on financial estimates that contained obvious deficiencies.

These inconsistencies reflected, at least in part, the absence of clear goals, other than the creation of more unitaries. Indeed, the government went as far as to admit that the review was 'a window of opportunity' to create unitary councils. But to what purpose? There were no plans for a continuing programme of structural change. Because there was no blueprint for the future, those involved in the process were often uncertain as to what was expected of them.

Because of these and many other shortcomings, the decisions reached by the government were not backed by clear and consistent judgements, nor any review of independent research. The decision letters reveal muddled and contradictory thinking, comparing one decision with another and even within decision letters. The authors' use of the term 'botched business' and their claim that 'parliament was misled and that there was a large element of political deception' (ibid., p.152) is consistent with the detail of their analysis.

What is clear is that the approach of the Banham Commission, which, whatever its limitations, was reasonably successful at meeting the four criteria used for evaluating the 2006–08 initiative, was not then replicated. By this time, there was sense that we were dealing with a 'solution in search of a problem'. Large unitary authorities were by now an idea whose time had come, at least as far as the DCLG were concerned. Rigorous comparative analysis of different structural options was not, and is still not, required or to be welcomed from outsiders, especially where they might conflict with the idea that 'bigger is better'. On this latter point a host of contradicting independent research findings have been overlooked or simply ignored as inconvenient (see for a small example: Blom-Hansen et al., 2016; Vakkala & Leinonen, 2016; Dollery & Keiichi, 2018; Erlingsson et al., 2020; Kalcheva, 2021; Vabo et al., 2021). We present a fuller analysis of this data which contradicts the 'bigger is better' mantra in Chap. 8.

The Unitary Bandwagon Rolls on 2015–22

After the five-year interregnum when Eric Pickles resisted departmental influence to reorganise local government on a unitary basis, there was again a period of frequent ministerial change, Greg Clark, Sajid Javid and David Brokenshire all enjoying relatively short periods of office as Secretary of State or local government minister at DCHLG. It is unlikely to have been a coincidence that it was during these periods of ministerial instability that reorganisation reappeared on the department's policy agenda. Three months after becoming Secretary of State, Sajid Javid proclaimed at a meeting of the County Councils Network (a vocal and vociferous supporter of unitary county-based local government) his belief that unitary authorities of population between 300,000 and 500,000 should be established across the country. One wonders where this commitment and the estimated population figure could possibly have come from! Why would an incoming minister with no previous experience of the world of local government, no record of speaking out on local government matters, and quite likely, little personal interest in it, think it a good idea to launch a local government reorganisation, unless prompted or encouraged to do so by departmental staff?

In what is now a predictable pattern, Simon Clarke, the incoming minister for local government in the Johnson administration, following the 2019 election, soon began to make public statements expressing enthusiasm for large unitary authorities of broadly the same size as those favoured by one of his predecessors, Sajid Javid, a few years earlier (see above). It has often seemed that the then DCHLG was seeking to identify an 'ideal size' for the new unitary authorities that it wished to see spread across the country. Was 300,000 too small? 500,000 too large? The idea that appropriate size might vary, depending on a variety of local circumstances, and that the search for the 'ideal size' could be seen as akin to a search for the 'philosophers' stone' (Newton, 1982) did not appear to occur to them. Nor did that the idea that the two-tier system, for all its perceived shortcomings, might offer much more flexibility seeking to match different sizes to different functions (strategic, larger: local, smaller) than a uniform system of large unitary authorities. Simon Clark resigned after a mere six months in the job and Secretary of State Robert Jenrick put the reorganisation process on hold in September 2020, as the Covid pandemic intensified (see Chap. 6). But, if our hypothesis is correct, senior DCHLG local government officials will be waiting for the next opportunity to reintroduce it and with Michael Gove making a return to the department as minister in 2022, that time may well have come again.. The consistency of the advocacy of unitarisation of local government is why it is so important to subject the arguments for large unitary authorities to critical scrutiny, which is the main task of the remaining chapters of this book.

What lies behind the DCHLG's long-term commitment to large unitary authorities? 'Administrative convenience' is the most plausible explanation. A uniform pattern of large unitary authorities would be much easier to deal with than the existing, more complex system involving two tiers of government in many of the county areas. This argument of 'administrative convenience' would also be relevant for other departments of state (Education, DHSS) as well as for DLUHC in relation to the levelling up agenda. That justification cannot of course be publicly acknowledged, although we have heard civil servants say so in private (and note a reported exchange between a senior civil servant and a local authority chief executive to this effect (see Chisholm & Leach, 2008, p 144)).

In an appearance in 2016 before the Public Administration Select Committee, the director general of the DCHLG Jo Farrar claimed that 'moving to a unitary system would provide a more streamlined service to the public'. It is unusual for a civil servant to prove so partisan about an issue that is, in essence, one of political choice; but her evidence only confirmed what has been apparent for many years, namely that there is a civil service agenda pushing for a system of this nature, which we strongly suspect has been recommended to a long succession of incoming ministers. The main argument put forward by Jo Farrar and other proponents of a move to large unitary authorities, with a vested interest in such a move, is the familiar 'economies of scale' platitude; that such a move would result in more efficient and (possibly) effective services and would save money. There is no evidence that consistently and clearly supports this view (and the Banham Commission certainly was not convinced by the claim). There are also diseconomies of scale, which increase the larger the proposed authority becomes which are overlooked in the debate. What would be needed to prove such claims would be a post-hoc, rigorous and independent examination of the financial and quality impact of a change of this nature, none of which, so far as we are aware, exist.

But even if credible evidence to support such a view were to be produced, it would not justify the systematic introduction of large unitary authorities. Jo Farrar's reference to 'more streamlined services to the public' is the giveaway phrase. It implies that the overriding purpose of local authorities is to provide public services and if these can be provided more economically by large unitary authorities, that clinches the argument—except that it doesn't. It involves a misrepresentation of the role of local authorities. They are not merely service-providing authorities. They are governmental institutions with responsibilities for the social, economic and environmental well-being of the residents of the areas they serve, in a way which transcends their service functions. They are 'place-shaping' agencies, to quote a term from the Lyons Report of 2007. Yet, place-shaping makes so much more sense when it is applied to places with a real sense of community identity and local loyalties. Before austerity pushed many authorities into a crisis/survival mode of operation, vision documents abounded. But visions for Cambridge, Norwich or Preston have much more resonance than visions for non-places such as Cheshire East, North Northamptonshire or Tameside.

There is an irony in that, in its eagerness to create large unitary authorities in the shire areas, the DLUHC appears to have lost sight of the fact that a two-tier system of local government has recently been re-created in the six former metropolitan county areas and four other locations. These 'combined authorities' are headed by an elected mayor, but otherwise comprise the leaders of the metropolitan district councils within the area, which remain in existence. This combined authority approach embodies recognition that there is indeed value in the two-tier principle: an upper tier for strategic planning, highways, public transport and economic development functions and another tier for local personal and environmental services. Such a division of responsibility would make equal sense in many other parts of England, for example Humberside, and the Portsmouth/ Southampton conurbation. Yet the DCHLG persists with its preference for large unitary authorities, unaware (or uninterested) in the fact that almost all Western democracies operate with two or in some cases three levels of local government (OECD, 2016).

Local democracy matters. We dilute it or ignore it at our peril. Before the 1974 reorganisation took place, there were 1430 local authorities in England, most of them representing real places. Within them, around 55,000 councillors carried out their duties. In 2020, there are 331 councils and around 17,500 councillors, with further significant falls in numbers likely in future in both categories, if present trends continue. Both current figures set us apart from other European countries, where the average size of local authorities is invariably far lower and the councillors per head of population ratio much higher. It is just not credible to regard authorities such as Cheshire East or Cornwall as in any meaningful sense 'local'.

Conclusion

The unitary principle that has become a long-standing part of the centre's thinking about local government can be characterised as an unfortunate expedient; unfortunate, in that it is based on a selective and unbalanced use of evidence, which ignores the conclusions from a wide range of academic studies (see Chap. 8).

Unitarisation can be viewed as an expedient because the policy is designed to meet the needs of the centre for administrative convenience and enhanced central control of local government; rather than those of local government and the communities within it. It is also an expedient in that it is based on a myopic view of the place of local government in the governing system which emphasises 'service delivery' rather than a genuine governmental function. In our view, it is highly likely that local government will see more territorial upheaval over the coming decades, resulting from the fact that unitarisation has become the 'conventional wisdom', fuelled by three decades of advocacy from an inflexible departmental mindset. In Chap. 6 we examine how, since 2019, the local government clock has ticked closer to a Doomsday scenario, in which it will hardly merit the label of LOCAL government. But first, the strange case of the 2018 Northamptonshire reorganisation.

References

Blom-Hansen, J., Houlberg, K., Serritzlew, S., & Treisman, D. (2016). Jurisdiction size and local government policy expenditure: Assessing the effect of municipal amalgamation. *American Political Science Review, 110*(4), 812–831.

Chisholm, M., & Leach, S. (2008). *Botched business: The damaging process of re-organising local government, 2006-2008.* Douglas McLean.

Department of Communities and Local Government. (2006). *Strong and prosperous communities.* cm 6939-1.

Dollery, B., & Keiichi, Y. (2018). Is bigger really better? A comparative analysis of municipal mergers in Australian and Japanese local government. *International Journal of Public Administration, 41*(9), 725–734.

Erlingsson, G. Ó., Ödalen, J., & Wångmar, E. (2020). How coerced municipal amalgamations thwart the values of local self-government. *Urban Affairs Review, 57*, 1–26.

Kalcheva, D. (2021). Territorial reforms in Bulgaria: The cases of municipal divorces, Ch7, 117–140. In M. Lackowska, K. Szmigiel-Rawska, & F. Teles (Eds.), *Local government in Europe: New perspectives and democratic challenges.* Bristol University Press.

Lyons, M. (2007). *Lyons inquiry into local government: Final report.* The Stationery Office.

Newton, K. (1982). Is small really so beautiful? Is big really so ugly? Size, effectiveness and democracy in local government. *Political Studies, 30*(2), 190–206.

OECD, & United Cities and Local Government (UCLG). (2016). *Subnational governments around the world structure and finance: A first contribution to the Global Observatory on Local Finances.*

Vabo, S., Fimreite, A. L., & Houlberg, K. (2021). Why such a different choice of tools? Analysing recent local government reforms in Denmark and Norway. *Local Government Studies.* https://doi.org/10.1080/03003930.2021.2013210

Vakkala, H., & Leinonen, J. (2016). Current features and developments of local governance in Finland: The changing roles of citizens and municipalities. In U. Sadioglu & K. Dede (Eds.), *Theoretical foundations and discussions on the reformation process in local governments* (Advances in Public Policy and Administration (APPA) Book Series) (pp. 304–328). Information Science Reference, IGI Global.

CHAPTER 5

A Strange Affair: Local Government Reorganisation in Northamptonshire 2018–21—A Case Study

Abstract The reorganisation in Northamptonshire in 2018, which resulted in the existing system of a county and seven districts being abolished and replaced by two new unitary authorities, provides further evidence for our hypothesis (see Chap. 4). The county was experiencing a financial crisis and a 'best value' review was instigated. In previous examples of financial mismanagement in other authorities, independent commissioners had been appointed and had succeeded in putting the authorities concerned back on a secure financial footing. In this case, although commissioners were appointed as a short-term response, the report of the review recommended the reorganisation summarised above. A structural recommendation of this nature to deal with a financial crisis is unprecedented. A detailed analysis of the sequence of events involved suggests a further successful piece of opportunism on the part of the government to further its 'large unitary authority' agenda (see Chap. 4).

Keywords Local government reorganisation • Structural change • Unitary council • County council • District councils • Best value • Failing authorities • County-district relations • Community identity

S. Leach, C. Copus, *The Strange Demise of the Local in Local Government*, Palgrave Studies in Sub-National Governance,
https://doi.org/10.1007/978-3-031-32819-0_5

Introduction

In this chapter we present a case study of a particular local government reorganisation. We have selected the reorganisation of local government in Northamptonshire, as it is one of the most recent completed reorganisations that occured while the book was being written and because it provides evidence of the opportunism of central government in pursuing its policy of establishing large unitary authorities in the shire counties, wherever possible, in this case altering the rules of the game to achieve this outcome.

The case study is divided into four parts. In the first part we examine the background to the reorganisation process. We go on to explore the origins of the Best Value Review of Northamptonshire instigated by the government in January 2018. In doing so, we highlight the recent history of county–district relations in the area, the attitudes of the county and districts to a move to unitary authorities and the worsening financial situation of the county from 2013 onwards.

In the second section, we examine the progress of the 2018 Best Value Review (The Caller Review) and critically evaluate the content of its March 2018 report, which recommended (inter alia) the replacement of the existing two-tier system of local government with two unitary authorities—North and West Northamptonshire—with populations of around 359,000 and 426,000 respectively.

Thirdly, we assess the reactions to the report from the different agencies involved and comment on the progress and impact of the move to the two unitary models. Finally, we seek to develop an explanation for the unprecedented recommendation (and implementation) of a structural reorganisation of local government as a 'solution' to a financial crisis in a local authority. There have been numerous financial crises identified in local authorities since the 1980s, but this is the first time this form of response has been advocated. It was indeed a 'strange affair'.

The Background

The stability of the two-tier system in shire counties was undermined by the establishment of the Banham Commission in 1991 and the expectation (largely unfulfilled) that it would lead to the widespread introduction of unitary authorities. Further opportunities were provided by the 2006–08 'bidding system' initiative of the Labour government. Throughout this period, the ambitions of Northamptonshire County Council (NCC) to achieve unitary status have been apparent. In 2006, the council prepared a pre-emptive bid of this nature without consulting the district councils. The proposal was never submitted, probably due to the lack of consultation with partners and stakeholders, but it was criticised by the districts and exacerbated the already problematic nature of the relationship between the county and district councils.

In response to NCC's unilateral action, the four district councils in the north of the county (Corby, Kettering, Wellingborough and East Northants) began to establish close working relationships over a range of local services, including planning and economic development, an initiative which had been identified by the Department for Leveling-up, Housing and Communities (DLUHC) as a possible alternative to a move to unitary authorities. In a sense, this could be seen as a district-inspired pre-emptive strike against future county bids for unitary status, as well as a contribution to more cost-effective local government in the north of the county. When the unitary agenda was revived in 2016, the four districts concerned submitted a proposal for a combined authority. This proposal was rejected by the then local government minister Greg Clark, mainly because of the reluctance of the four authorities to accept an elected mayor as part of their proposal, but also because the minister by then seemed more committed to the idea of large unitary authorities in the shire counties. When the budgetary crisis in the NCC began to become apparent from 2013 onwards, the possibility of local government reorganisation in the county, although never seen as a likely response to the problem, was nevertheless there in the background as an influence on attitudes.

The developing budgetary crisis in NCC had been confirmed by two adverse 'value for money' reports from KPMG, the council's auditors in 2015–16 and 2016–17 and by a critical peer review, carried out by the LGA in 2017. It was clear that the 'Next Generation Council' strategy, initiated in 2012 and which involved an emphasis on the outsourcing of a wide range of council services to external providers, managed by a streamlined strategic commissioning core, was not achieving the anticipated savings. Criticism built up from the district councils and from the county's M.P.s, all of whom were Conservatives and who were receiving numerous complaints from their constituents regarding NCC's perceived inability to manage its financial affairs.

Within NCC, there was increasing unease and criticism, not just from opposition members, but from backbench members of the Conservative majority party. Jason Smithers, elected in February 2018 for the Higham

Ferres ward, was reprimanded later that year by the authority's Standards Committee for offensive tweets, issued shortly after his election, directed at the council's leader Heather Smith and the Finance portfolio holder Robin Brown, in which he appeared to be suggesting that the Serious Fraud Squad should be called in (although he later denied this). The atmosphere at the time was described as 'poisonous' by one of our interviewees with the county's Conservative MPs aligning themselves with NCC's internal and external critics, rather than seeking to support the authority's Conservative cabinet.

The Best Value Review

It was into this conflict-ridden environment that the then DCHLG decided to commission a Best Value review of NCC. The Review team, appointed on January 9, 2018, was led by Max Caller, a former London Borough Chief Executive and a lead commissioner for best value interventions, and also included Julie Parker, who had been a member of the LGA peer review in 2017. It was required to report by March 15, 2022. The terms of reference required the team to evaluate NCC's performance on the basis of six criteria, all concerned with NCC's culture and capacity to manage its finances effectively, and which included the following (DCHLG, 2018, p.3)

- consideration of whether NCC has the right culture, governance and processes to make robust decisions on resource allocation and to plan and manage its finances effectively
- consideration of its organisational and structural approaches to securing value for money and whether it is organised appropriately to ensure value for money in the delivery of its functions.
- does the county council have strong processes in place to manage services within budgetary constraints, within the council's finance department and also within service areas?

Nowhere in the brief was there any reference to a structural reorganisation of local government in the county being a relevant consideration or possible 'solution'.

During the review period, there were three new developments which clearly influenced the review team's conclusions and recommendations. On February 2, the county's Section 151 officer issued a Section 114 notice which warned that '*the council was at risk of not being able to balance its budget by the year's end and which imposed spending conditions to attempt to remedy the situation*'. On February 20, the council's auditors KPMG issued an advisory notice stating that '*it believed that the council was about to set an illegal budget*'. Both these developments had the effect of accentuating the sense of crisis and of questioning the competence of the administration to deal with it. The third development was a change in the regulations regarding the use of capital receipts to fund review spending, which effectively precluded NCC's plan to sell and then lease back its headquarters at One Angel Square, a transaction which would have generated around £50 million in capital receipts. This decision was important, because the council's hope was that, if this plan went ahead, it would offer a short-term solution to enable it to balance the books in 2018–19 and the subsequent year.

The team's report, published on March 21, 2018, was a damning indictment of NCC's budgetary and financial management processes since 2013–14. It addressed the arguments the county council had made to explain its difficulties, but gave them little credibility, less so than they perhaps merited (DCHLG, 2018, pp16–19 and 36). NCC had argued that the financial settlement had received each year since 2013–14 from the government was particularly punishing, compared with that received by almost all other shire counties. It had not taken account of the county's increasing population and its high proportion of elderly people, which had major consequences for the social care budget. The review team was unimpressed. It was also unimpressed by the council's adherence to the 'Next Generation Council' strategy, despite the fact that a significant number of other Conservative-controlled councils had adopted a similar 'outsourcing' approach (compatible with Conservative government's advice since the 1980s). This approach is difficult to modify in the short-term, because of the contractual obligations involved with external service providers. Although the Caller report was thorough and well-researched, it gave the impression to outside observers of a 'hatchet job'—a one-sided indictment of the council's shortcomings with little or no attempt to take into account the council's particular problems and arguments.

After 35 pages of critical analysis, the expectation of many was that the report would recommend that commissioners should be appointed by central government, to remedy its budgetary and financial management shortcomings, until such time as they were satisfied that the council was capable of managing its own finances competently. This was the remedy that was applied to several 'failing councils' under the Best Value regime instituted by the Labour government in 2000. The outcome was always that the commissioners were able to withdraw after (at most) a couple of years, with the authorities concerned back on an even keel. This was the outcome which was advocated by the county's Conservative M.P.s, in a joint statement in February 2018, issued soon after the review was announced (a review which it is highly likely they had been influential in persuading DCHLG to set up).

But no! The report concluded that 'the problems faced by NCC were so deep and ingrained that it is not possible to promote a recovery plan that would bring the council back to stability and safety in a reasonable timescale' (ibid. p36). It went on to argue that to change the culture and organisational ethos of the council and to restore balance would (in the judgement of the inspection team) take of the order of five years and require a substantial one-off cash injection. Effectively, it would be a reward for failure.

The report concluded (ibid. pp37–8) that 'a way forward' with a 'clean sheet' was required. Its key recommendation was that this should involve the abolition of the existing two-tier system and its replacement by two unitary authorities (North and West Northamptonshire) with populations of 359,000 and 426,000 respectively. What this plan meant was that the district councils that were not performing poorly were to be abolished and merged because of the problems of the much larger county council.

The argument that a recovery plan of some description was not in itself a viable option is highly contentious. Recovery plans, supported by outside direction, have worked successfully in several other authorities, including some whose problems seemed at the time as severe as those experienced by NCC (e.g. Walsall in 2002, Tower Hamlets in 2014 and Liverpool in 2021). Changes in leadership, at political or senior management level or both, have been effective in turning failing authorities round in a year or so, a time scale far short of the five years predicted in the Caller report. The possibilities of such changes were never addressed in the report nor was the probability that many of the NCC councillors judged to be so incompetent would find their way on to the two new authorities.

The large cash injection claimed to be necessary was never required; by the end of the 2019–20 financial year, NCC, under new leadership and with the help of commissioners (appointed in the summer of 2018) had emerged from the financial crisis and succeeded in balancing the books without the benefit of this input. The sale and lease back of One Angel

Square had been permitted to go ahead and helped in this remedial process. In 2018–19, there was actually an underspend in the council's budget. The argument that the position in NCC could not be remedied by measures other than a costly, time-consuming and unnecessary local government reorganisation was premature and difficult, in retrospect, to justify.

In their report, the inspectors used as part of their justification for the 'fresh start' recommendation a summary of the views of district leaders regarding the culture of NCC and the problems of changing it. It claimed that district council leaders believed that it was not possible to ensure effective partnership working with NCC: that there was a level of doubt that NCC would ever be able to deliver against its promises and undertakings: and that whilst most district leaders preferred the status quo, they thought that what mattered was the best result for the people of the county and that some form of unitary government was now thought to be the only possible solution that the government would accept.

There is no reason to question the first two claims, although in each case, the proviso 'under its current leadership' could reasonably have been inserted. But the third claim is more surprising. Without access to the interview transcripts (if indeed these exist) it is impossible to know the precise nature of the relevant exchanges. Was this view volunteered by district leaders or was it a response to a (possibly loaded) question which raised the possibility that a move to unitary authorities was 'the only possible solution'. Certainly, all the district leaders and other senior politicians we interviewed expressed surprise when this was the recommendation which emerged, which would not have been the case had this option been clearly signalled in the interviews. There is a grey area here; the implication that widespread support for a unitary solution was expressed by district leaders during the interview process seems unlikely or at least debatable.

However, one council leader, when he learned that Max Caller was to be the lead inspector, did see this outcome as a possibility. In 2008, the leader of the District Councils Network was from a Norfolk district. In the 2006–08 reorganisation initiative, Norwich's bid for unitary status was referred to the Boundary Commission, who were asked to widen their remit to cover the whole county. The lead commissioner was Max Caller whose team recommended a unitary county, in a situation in which this option was difficult to justify. Indeed, one of the authors of this book was commissioned by the district councils to provide a critique of the unitary county proposal. The critique identified a wide range of untenable assumptions and questionable reasoning in the proposal, which was not implemented, as the incoming Conservative/Liberal Democrat coalition in 2010 called a halt to all forms of reorganisation. But Max Caller's reputation as an enthusiast for large unitary authorities had become apparent.

The Best Value review had been formally initiated by Sajid Javid, shortly after he had been appointed as Communities minister. No doubt his action had been based on civil service advice (and lobbying from the county's Conservative MPs). It was no surprise when he announced acceptance of the Inspection Team's recommendations. The MPs were unanimous in their support for the abolition of NCC. But there was one obstacle in the way of implementation. There was at the time no legislation which required local authorities to move from a two-tier to a unitary system. This outcome could only result if the authorities concerned submitted a bid to DCHLG requesting a change of this nature. It appeared that the ball was back in the court of NCC and the districts.

The Response to the Caller Report

In principle, the county council and the district councils, acting collectively, could have refused to submit a bid for a move to a unitary outcome, although had they done so, the government would no doubt have found an alternative way of enforcing it. It is not surprising that that a path of non-compliance was not followed. It would have been unpopular with a significant proportion of the county's residents, who had become accustomed to critical media reports of NCC's failings. The seven Conservative MPs would have been outraged, and given their influence in the county, could have made things very difficult for Conservative leaders who dug their heels in.

The only serious resistance came from Corby. Corby's leader was not opposed to unitary authorities in principle, but he could not understand what the justification was for the preferred population size of 300,000–400,000, which was being advocated by DCHLG at the time (his justifiable concerns are addressed in the final section of this case study). After all, Rutland Unitary Authority, which shares a boundary with Corby, has a population of only 40,000 and there are other unitary authorities of equivalent size to Corby on Teeside. Nor were Corby happy with the timetable, which required the two new authorities to be up and running by May 2020 and which was felt to provide too short a time to ensure a robust, workable outcome. They were proved right; the launch of the new councils was later postponed until May 2021. An opinion poll of residents, conducted by the council, revealed that 95% of the local population opposed the unitary plans and wanted Corby to remain a local authority, a result which cut no ice with the inspection team.

The other leaders in the North Northamptonshire districts, however unhappy they were about the disappearance from the local government map of the town-based councils they represented and proud of what their councils had achieved, felt that they had little choice but to accept the recommendations of the Caller report. The pressure from local MPs, the difficulties of challenging the financial analysis and conclusions of what appeared to be a very thorough report and the knowledge that there was a tradition of co-operation amongst the four districts which they could build upon in the proposed new authority all played a part in their judgement. And to argue against the disappearance of the county, about which they had been so critical, would have seemed inconsistent. By the summer of 2018, all the authorities with the exception of Corby had voted for their own extinction. The requisite application to DCHLG to implement the two unitary proposals was made and work began, through the mechanism of Joint Committees of county and district councillors, to prepare for the establishment of North and West Northamptonshire in 2020. Corby Borough Council, understandably wishing to ensure that its interests were protected in this process, ended its stand-off later in 2018 and became an active participant.

When it became clear that the transition could not be achieved in two years, that the 'shadow authorities' in North and West Northamptonshire would need to operate until May 2021 and that the county council would need to continue in operation as a local authority (as would the seven districts) for a period of three years, the question was raised as to how successful the county council would be in resolving its financial problems over this extended period. The answer was that it did so with a reasonable degree of success. With new political leadership, a new management team and the involvement of the two appointed commissioners, NCC made impressive progress. The books were balanced and a legal budget set for the 2018–19 financial year (despite KPMG's fears) and over the three year period, good progress was made in turning the authority round. A substantial financial input was not required, contrary to the expectations of the Inspection team. In the light of these developments, it is a moot point whether NCC was the 'hopeless case' which the Inspectors considered it to be and whether the 'nuclear option' of a wholesale reorganisation was in fact necessary.

The problems faced by NCC during the years of austerity have not gone away. In the county's 'Mind the Gap' analysis, the growing disparity between the needs of a growing elderly population and the resources available to meet these needs was highlighted. This problem has remained; indeed, it has worsened, as the two new unitary authorities soon discovered. One of our interviewees likened the reorganisation to 'cutting the Titanic in half', a metaphor which has a good deal of resonance. It is too soon to judge whether the introduction of two new unitary authorities in the county will prove to be of real benefit to its inhabitants, but, as we argue in the final section, there are grounds for serious doubts.

Explaining the 'Strange Affair' of the Abolition of NCC

The process which led to the introduction of the two unitary authorities in Northamptonshire was deeply flawed. A whole range of considerations which are normally addressed in assessing the case for a move from two-tier local government to a unitary system were ignored. In previous cases, a detailed analysis of the cost implications of moving from one option to the other had always been carried out, including an assessment of the transitional costs, which have typically been assessed in previous county-based reorganisations at around £25 million. This analysis was inexplicably omitted in the Caller review. All that the report provided was a forecast of a substantial (but unspecified) one-off payment to NCC if it continued in existence (which was later shown not to be required). At the very least, an estimate of the transitional costs should have been made and an attempt to explain how these costs would be balanced by the savings involved in the move to a two unitary option. The possibility that the substantial one-off payment predicted by the inspection team might be avoided (which turned out to be the case) should also have been taken into account.

Second, no attempt was made to assess the impact of the change on the pattern of community identity in the county. Evidence from the Banham

Commission county reports indicated that the highest level of community identity was with towns (small and large), which was a key factor in the Commission deciding not to recommend the introduction of unitary authorities in the majority of the shire counties. The public opinion survey in Corby revealed a large majority (95%) favoured the retention of Corby BC. It is likely that similar results would have emerged in Wellingborough, Kettering and Daventry, all free-standing towns with long civic traditions and indeed in the city of Northampton itself. Local democracy works most effectively when there is a link between the definition of a local authority and a strong local community identity. For this reason, the loss of the five councils identified above is to be regretted. It is highly unlikely North and West Northamptonshire will ever inspire an equivalent level of community identity, given that they are in effect arbitrary amalgamations of real places. Considerations of community identity and public opinion should have been included in the Caller report, but were conspicuous by their absence.

Third, there was a further detrimental impact on the quality of local democracy which received no coverage in the Caller report. England already has by far the highest councillor-to-population ratio of any Western democracy There is ample evidence of the considerable time demands currently experienced by councillors—executive and 'backbench'—in two-tier counties, if they are to carry out their roles effectively. The impact of the move from two-tier to unitary government in Northamptonshire was to reduce the number of councillors in the county from around 400 to 150, a reduction of 60%. This has placed an increased pressure on councillors, many of whom had already claimed to be overworked. This reduction weakens the local democratic process. Its omission from the Caller report is hard to justify.

Fourth, in its identification of unitary options, the Caller report provides no justification for the limited scope for choice which it offered. Unsurprisingly, the possibility of a unitary county was dismissed, as was the option of a unitary Northampton as the 'hole in the doughnut' of a unitary residual county. The councils were ultimately faced with a non-choice: North and West Northamptonshire, with populations in the range 360,000–425,000, which coincided conveniently with DCHLG's view, echoed by the then newly appointed Secretary of State Sajid Javid, that the range 300,000–400,000 was the most appropriate size for a unitary authority.

But where did this figure come from? The answer appears to be from the top of the head of someone in DCHLG. There has never been—in the Caller report or elsewhere—a justification for the range quoted. If one studies the size distribution of unitary authorities in England, there are many examples of populations below 175,000, half the currently favoured figure. On Teeside, the average size of the unitary authorities is 140,000: in what used to be Berkshire it is 153,000. Unitary Rutland (population 40,000) was so designated in 1992 on account of the strength of its local community identity. The case for a unitary Corby, Kettering or Wellingborough might also be seen as a persuasive one, on this basis.

How is this 'strange affair' to be explained? There are no precedents for what happened in Northamptonshire. There had been a couple of county-based reorganisations since 2015 (Dorset in 2019 where two unitaries were created, and Buckinghamshire which became a unitary county after the abolition of the district councils in 2020) but in neither case was financial mismanagement on the part of one of the authorities concerned cited as a justification for the change. In the brief provided for the Best Value review of NCC, there was no mention of the possibility of a possible reorganisation being on the agenda. Nor were the county's Conservative MPs pushing publicly for this option at the time of the Best Value review.

Neither author has much time for 'conspiracy theory' explanations for unexpected policy decisions. But in reviewing a range of possible explanations for what happened, we found the following scenario to be the most convincing. The predilection of the DCHLG Local Government Unit for large unitary authorities is long established and well known. With the exception of Eric Pickles, a succession of newly appointed Secretaries of State—both Conservative and Labour—have gone on record in support of this policy, no doubt well briefed by the LG unit. Opportunities have been sought throughout the 2000–21 period to introduce new unitary authorities. In our view, it is likely NCC's financial crisis was seen as one such opportunity. The appointment of Max Caller as lead inspector is likely to have been a further explanatory factor. His enthusiasm for large unitary authorities is well known (see, e.g., his role in Norfolk in 2008, discussed in the previous section). He had undertaken various projects for DCHLG and is clearly seen as a reliable ally, with sound beliefs and values. We have no evidence that he was briefed informally by DCHLG to make the recommendation which he did; but this might well not have been perceived to be necessary. His track record on unitary local government spoke for itself.

No doubt other explanations are possible. But until such time as one is produced with a greater level of plausibility, we would see our interpretation as a viable hypothesis which fits the facts and sequence of events which we have outlined in this case study.

Reference

DCHLG. (2018). *Best value report on Northamptonshire County Council.*

CHAPTER 6

Doomsday Approaches and then Recedes

Abstract Early in 2020, following the Conservative general election victory of December 2019, a new reorganisation initiative was announced which would abolish the two-tier local government in the shire counties where it still operated and replace it with unitary authorities with populations of 300,000 and above. Unsubstantiated arguments were made that this would somehow contribute to government's 'levelling up agenda'. Work commenced in the counties concerned, but was halted later that year by Robert Jenrick, the Secretary of State concerned, when the scale of the Covid epidemic became apparent, although the process was permitted to go ahead in Somerset, North Yorkshire and Cumbria. There was however a retreat signalled by the Minister, who emphasised in a letter to local authority Conservative leaders that there would be no more 'top down' reorganisation imposed by Whitehall. It is likely that this change of policy direction was influenced by many Conservative MPs who were resistant to the prospect of a structural upheaval in their constituencies. But opportunities are likely to be sought to reintroduce this measure when the time is judged to be right.

Keywords Local government reorganisation • Levelling up • Value for money • Devolution • Local government improvement • Public sector reform • Service delivery • Combined authority • Economies of scale

S. Leach, C. Copus, *The Strange Demise of the Local in Local Government*, Palgrave Studies in Sub-National Governance, https://doi.org/10.1007/978-3-031-32819-0_6

Introduction

In Chap. 4 we explored and sought to explain the persistence of the unitary principle in the thinking of the central department concerned with local government, currently known as the Department for Levelling Up, Housing and Communities (DLUHC). That persistence reflects a technocratic view of the role of local government, focused on efficient and effective service delivery, and a disregard of the importance of communities of place. Following the 1969 Redcliffe-Maud report the introduction of the term 'unitary' into the lexicon of local government became a touchstone for departmental thinking. Linked to the unitary principle is the equally persistent and consistent thinking that the size of local government units should increase and that larger-scale local government is unquestionably more efficient and effective than the smaller-scale alternative.

In this chapter we examine how the centre's tendency to link new policy initiatives to local government reorganisation has been illustrated through 'levelling up', the 2019 Conservative government's plan to redistribute wealth and stimulate economic activity across the country. In doing so, we question the relevance of further local government reorganisation to the aims of 'levelling up'. We go on to look at one particular example of reorganisation which has been instigated since 2019: Cumbria in the North West of England.

Local Government Reorganisation and Levelling Up

In the spring of 2020, with the first wave of the Covid pandemic apparently over in England (but not for long), a local government reorganisation was launched which must have delighted the enthusiasts for large unitary authorities within the senior management of the DCHLG, and which, if our hypothesis is accepted, they would have played a major role in stimulating. As noted in Chap. 4, this agenda was tacked on to the government's stated aim of extending devolution beyond the Northern Powerhouse combined authorities' initiative (several of which are not located in the North!) as an impetus to post-Covid economic regeneration, particularly in the 'red wall' constituencies where 'levelling up' was viewed as a priority.

A Devolution White Paper was scheduled for late-2020 but was not published until early 2022 (DLUHC, 2022). But authorities in the shire counties which still operated a two-tier system were given the go-ahead to begin discussions aimed at putting forward and hopefully agreeing proposals for unitary local government. The option of the retention of a two-tier system was explicitly excluded.

How a major reorganisation of this nature was supposed to contribute to the broader aims of 'levelling up' and economic regeneration was never made clear. The 'levelling up' concept has, from its inception, been suffused with vagueness; a vagueness which the almost 300 page long white paper failed to disperse. However, what the white paper did very successfully clarify was the government's view that two-tier local government was seen as part of 'fragmentation and administrative complexity' of the landscape of the public sector. That fragmentation and complexity, the white paper maintained, had been streamlined in Scotland and Wales through single-tier local government (DLUHC, 2022:133). In total, the white paper's contents do not justify the claims of a 'revolution in local democracy' promised in the then Prime Minister's forward, as there are no new freedoms, autonomy or real powers for local government.

The expectations surrounding local government reorganisation had earlier been clarified in a series of ministerial statements early in 2020:

> We need to move towards a model that provides better value for money for taxpayers and able to look more strategically at challenges like housing and transport (Robert Jenrick)

Terms like 'better value for money' and 'strategy' are invariably precursors of commitments to large unitary authorities, a link made more explicit in a statement from local government minister Simon Clarke.

> The Government recognises that unitary councils can facilitate more integrated decision-making, better service delivery and empowerment of local communities.

He added (in case anyone was in any doubt) 'the unitarisation of counties is a vital first step in negotiating devolution deals in the future'; clearly the words of someone who had bought into the departmental mind-set and done so extremely quickly!

Various population figures regarding the 'ideal size' for these proposed new unitary authorities were banded about, with the government at one stage specifying a minimum size of 300,000. This was not necessarily good news for the County Councils Network (CCN), the majority of whose members had populations well above that figure; indeed, in six counties the population was over a million. The implication was that in counties such as Kent, Lancashire and Essex, there might be as many as three or four new unitary authorities created (with the potential for yet more 'points of the compass' councils). It was not surprising, therefore, that in the various studies commissioned by the CCN to support their case, arguments were put forward claiming that the larger the new authorities the better.

Henham Strategy, in their report entitled (somewhat pretentiously) 'Making Counties Count; Weaving a new Tapestry for Local Government', state that *'we think the risks of having new unitary authorities which are too small is sufficiently worrying that this number (the 300,000 quoted above) is too low'* (Henham Strategy, 2020:34). Well they would, wouldn't they; consultants tend not to express views out of line with their clients' best interests! An earlier report by Shared Intelligence claimed that *'there is no doubt that larger councils, those with a higher population, are better placed to deliver economies of scale than smaller councils. Large populations should be mandatory for any new unitary.'* The CCN-sponsored reports by Price Waterhouse which provide estimates of potential savings generated by a move to large unitary authorities always conclude that the bigger the authority, the greater the savings—size is no object! Henham Strategy concur, posing the question of whether the six counties with populations of over a million are too big for a single unitary authority to govern well and concluding unsurprisingly, that 'we don't think so'.

It is important to note how little reference there was in these reports to what one would have thought were highly relevant concepts, such as the health of local democracy and the importance of local community. It often appeared that the potential for saving money and providing more cost-efficient and -effective services was the only criterion of significance in the debate.

Thus, in the summer of 2020, the battle lines were drawn, with the counties (through the CCN) commissioning and publishing several reports to back up their case for large unitary authorities (preferably based on existing counties). The districts, which are much less well-resourced than the counties, were fighting something of a rear-guard action. In general, they did not argue for the continuation of the two-tier system (much as many of them would have liked to) because the rules appeared to preclude this option. The main 'damage limitation' strategy was to argue for smaller unitary authorities, combining two or at most three district councils and seeking to derail the unitary county bandwagon.

In September, rumours began to emerge that the government was about to call a halt to the reorganisation process. In response, the CCN sent a letter to the prime minister, pleading with him not to do so. The content of the letter includes a suggestion that pressure from Conservative-controlled district councils could be influencing the Minister (CCN September 18, 2020).

> It is no surprise that so much of the vitriol aimed at Robert Jenrick for driving a unitary approach has come from those sources obsessed with self-protection above good governance and a chance to transform society for the better.

So, were the counties not also 'obsessed with self-protection'? The CCN's plea fell on deaf ears. Indeed, its tactics brought complaints from not only district councillors but some county councillors who thought it had overstepped the mark. On October 12, Robert Jenrick wrote to all the councils involved in the process to announce that the process was indeed to be halted. The reason given was that the energies of both central government and local authorities should be focused on dealing with the Covid pandemic, when there had recently been a sharp increase in the number of cases in England. This was an eminently sensible justification, but it was by no means the full story. The CCN had been right in their conjecture of 'behind the scenes' pressure, which had in fact come from backbench MPs, who were not happy with the direction the reorganisation was taking. It was not at all surprising that this should be the case. In the shire counties, a large number of parliamentary constituencies are co-terminous with district councils, the Conservative members of which typically play a supportive role to the local MP, both at election time and in the Constituency party in which they are usually dominant figures. They will, no doubt, have made their concerns about the likely disappearance of 'their district council' abundantly clear.

In a Ministerial Statement (House of Commons: October 12, 2020) and a subsequent letter to all Conservative councillors in England, the Minister indicated a major switch of policy, which offered some encouragement to those critical of the 'bigger is better' assumption and the dangers of central imposition of changes, the need for which was disputed amongst the authorities who would be affected. The letter set out the following principles:

- Improvements should be locally led. It is important that those seeking to pursue locally led proposals can demonstrate that there is broad local support for reform. It is up to local areas to decide whether or not they want to reform their structures.
- Improvements should not be compulsory or required. Unitary structures are not and will not be compulsory or required by central government. Any reform of an area's local government structure is most effectively achieved by those who best know the area.
- There should be no top-down restructuring. It should not involve Whitehall solutions being imposed on local areas.
- There are other ways of delivering reform. Joint working with other councils and partners could be an appropriate and sustainable way forward.

Three exceptions were made to this laissez-faire approach. Cumbria, North Yorkshire and Somerset had, it was claimed, been considering reform for some time and there was 'broad local support' for reform. These counties were invited to make outline proposals for reform to DCHLG by November 5. No other counties were invited to do so.

It remained to be seen what the government means by 'broad local support', a criterion which would be tested in the likely event of competing proposals being submitted in these three counties. And it is hard to believe that the 'large unitary authority' agenda which has been so persistent a feature of DCHLG policy for the past 25 years has disappeared for the foreseeable future, particularly when Robert Jenrick is replaced by Michael Gove who might well not feel bound by the assurances his predecessor has given. But for the moment, at least there was a pause for reflection, in which the doomsday scenario might come to be reconsidered.

The Cumbria Experience

The first test of the meaning of 'broad local support' emerged from the proposals put forward by the authorities in Cumbria in November 2020, which the government earmarked for 'a further round of consultation' in March 2021.

- Barrow, South Lakeland and Lancaster have jointly submitted a proposal for two unitary councils: 'The Bay' comprising the three areas they cover and 'North Cumbria' comprising the area covered by the four remaining Cumbrian councils—Carlisle, Eden, Allerdale and Copeland.

- Allerdale and Copeland have jointly submitted a proposal for a different two-way split: 'West Cumbria' (Carlisle, Allerdale and Copeland) and 'East Cumbria' (Barrow, Eden and South Lakes)
- Carlisle and Eden have jointly submitted a proposal dividing the county area into 'North Cumbria' (Allerdale, Carlisle and Eden) and South Cumbria (Barrow, Copeland and South Lakes)
- Cumbria County Council have submitted a proposal arguing for a single unitary authority—'One Cumbria' covering the whole of the county area.

The production of multiple reorganisation options was eminently predictable. Having all assumed (arguably wrongly) that a unitary system is inevitable, the authorities in Cumbria have done what you would have expected them to do; the county has argued for a unitary Cumbria, and the districts have formed alliances which they hope will deliver the 'least worst' option (from their perspectives). It is difficult to imagine how this diversity of response and preference could be construed as broad local support for anything, apart for some form of unitary system. Robert Jenrick made it clear (see above) that 'unitary structures are not and will not be compulsory or required by central government'. If, notwithstanding the transparent lack of 'broad local support' for any of the proposed options, one of them were to be given the go-ahead by the government, then the hollowness of Jenrick's pledges would become clear. If, however, he was prepared to acknowledge that a credible basis for moving to a unitary option did not exist, then there would be enhanced credibility regarding the principles he had set out.

The announcement of the government's decisions on the future of Cumbria, North Yorkshire and Somerset was made in February 2021. It was clear that the agenda of the local government section of DCHLG had prevailed and outweighed Jenrick's pledges. North Yorkshire (population 604,900) and Somerset (population 560,000) were to become unitary authorities. In Cumbria, however, two new unitary authorities were to be designated: West Cumbria (comprising the district council areas of Carlisle, Allerdale and Copeland, with a population of 250,000) and East Cumbria (comprising the district council areas of Barrow, South Lakeland and Eden, with a population of 250,000).

In North Yorkshire and Somerset, the Government had not been faced with the Cumbrian situation of four incompatible options on the table. In these counties, there was a straight choice between a unitary county and a division into two sub-divisions, the option submitted in each case by the districts. Although the public opinion survey commissioned by the Somerset districts had demonstrated a clear preference for their favoured option, the whole exercise lost credibility as a result of a link included on the survey form, which was critical of the unitary county option. Following previous precedents (Wiltshire, Shropshire, Buckinghamshire), a unitary Somerset was always a likely option despite a referendum in Somerset in 2007 returning an overwhelming 82% in favour of retaining the two-tier system during an earlier reorganisation battle—the government clearly had Somerset in its sights for some time and 15 years later over-rode public opinion.

Although a unitary North Yorkshire will become the largest in population size of all the non-urban unitaries (and indeed the largest in area—it is 110 miles between Whitby in the north-east of the county and Skipton in the south-west) there was no compelling socio-geographic reasons for sub-dividing it. It is worth noting that the population of a unitary North Yorkshire—604,900 and rising—is larger than that of the state of Wyoming (579,000) in the USA and approaching that of Vermont (624,000)' Wyoming has 176 units of local government within its boundaries (counties, districts and single purpose authorities) whilst North Yorkshire will soon have none. It will have town and parish councils, but their powers are much more limited than those of any of the units in Wyoming and, of course, do not cover the whole of North Yorkshire.

In Cumbria, as we have shown, there was not the remotest shred of evidence of a 'broad level of support' for any of the submitted options. The only credible conclusion which can be drawn is that the term 'broad level of support' was used by the DCHLG to refer to the principle of moving to a unitary structure (rather than retaining a two-tier system) in Cumbria, not to support for any particular option in Cumbria, which was conspicuous by its absence. As noted above, the progress that had been made in these three counties, which was used as a justification for exempting them from the reorganisation moratorium announced in November 2020, was more likely to have resulted from a growing sense among the authorities concerned, during the preceding months, that change was inevitable and that they might as well get on with the job. But even this assumption can be questioned. When the reorganisation initiative was launched in the spring of 2020, only Cumbria CC and the district councils of Allerdale and Copeland expressed support for a change to a unitary structure. The other four district councils—a majority of the local authorities in the area—argued against change. It is hard to understand how this arithmetic could be interpreted as a 'broad level of support' for a unitary structure. Later, Carlisle City Council did express support for the unitary principle, probably in anticipation of the inevitability of this outcome.

It was, of course, still possible for Robert Jenrick to have judged that the subsequent lack of agreement in Cumbria regarding the options meant that reorganisation could not be justified in the county. But this was not his decision, despite his assurance in his November 2020 Commons statement that *'there should be no top-down restructuring; it should not involve Whitehall solutions being imposed on local areas'*. In essence a 'Whitehall solution' did come to be imposed. Our hypothesis would be that pressure from the unit within the DCHLG which has responsibility for reorganisation and has for many years been seeking opportunities to introduce large unitary authorities (see Chap. 4), proved persuasive. It is unlikely that the Minister himself had strong (or indeed any) views about the future of local government in that county, although he may have noted the enthusiasm of two of the Cumbrian districts with a strong Conservative representation—Allerdale and Copeland (with a Conservative directly elected mayor)—for a unitary outcome.

But this was not the end of the story. Whereas in the other two counties, the ministerial decisions were not contested, in Cumbria an application has been made by the county council for a judicial review of the decision to go for an East/West split. The county must have confidently anticipated the award of unitary status, following such outcomes in Dorset and Buckinghamshire (and previously, Wiltshire, Shropshire and Cornwall). It drew attention to the inconsistency in the decisions made in the three counties involved in the 2020 exercise. If a unitary county could be justified in North Yorkshire and Somerset, then why not in Cumbria, whose population (500,000) is appreciable smaller than both counties.

To understand the potential strength of Cumbria CC's case, it is necessary to examine the reasoning behind the Government's decision. Three criteria which would be used to evaluate different proposals had been identified at the start of the process:

- Is the proposal likely to improve service delivery across the area concerned?

- Does it command a good deal of local support, as assessed in the round, across the whole area of the proposal?
- Will any unitary council to be established have a credible geography?

None of these criteria was subjected to any kind of rigorous analysis, apart from references to the results of the consultation exercise carried out by the government to assess local support. They remain at a level of generality ('credible geography'? 'a good deal of local support'?) which (conveniently) allows for a range of alternative interpretations. In the case of Cumbria, the 'decision letter', it was argued that the two unitary (East/West) proposal was to be preferred to a single unitary authority for the whole of Cumbria as *'it would allow for more balanced decision making, particularly important, given the physical geography of Cumbria'* (the reference to 'physical geography' presumably refers to the Lake District, a large mountainous area in the very centre of the county). The two other proposals are excluded (with little supporting explanation) because neither 'complied with a credible geography' and the Bay proposal *'would be unlikely to improve local services'*, a view strongly contested by its advocates, not least because it would have been co-terminous with the Morecambe Bay Health Authority. It should also be noted that it was the Bay proposal which received a much higher level of public support in the consultation exercise than any of the other options, thus leading the field in relation to the second criterion, an outcome of apparently little consequence to MCHLG.

In the light of this apology for serious comparative analysis, it is not surprising that Cumbria sought a judicial review. The grounds for doing so which they have highlighted are illegality, irrationality, procedural irregularities and *'legitimate expectations'*. Amongst the more detailed challenges to the basis for the decision, set out in the notice of application are the following:

- It failed to consistently consider the consultation responses of the county council, showing why two unitary authorities did not meet the Secretary of State's own guidance and would not deliver what his guidance required.
- It failed to recognise that the two unitary model is predicated around the creation of a mayoral combined authority to ensure co-ordination on key matters, thus adding a new tier of local government, undermining the savings claimed, the need for which was a key reason why a single unitary authority was appropriate.

- For no valid reason, it acted inconsistently with his decision in North Yorkshire, where a single unitary authority was adopted, for reasons equally applicable to Cumbria.
- It appears that the decision could have been motivated by the possible partisan political advantage that splitting Cumbria in two may secure for his party. If this were a factor in the decision, it would be an abuse of power and unlawful.

The last of these claims is the most contentious. It has been strenuously denied by DCHLG. But if the judicial review team had been able to uncover evidence for it, it would have been a huge embarrassment to the government. The point about the elected mayor/combined authority is a pertinent one. Given that the underlying basis for the reorganisation is a dissatisfaction with the existing two-tier system, it seems inconsistent to require it to be replaced by an alternative version of two-tier local government, which is indeed what would be involved by the creation of a county-wide mayoral authority.

The judicial review did not find in the county's favour; nor did the appeal which the county subsequently lodged against the judge's decision. As a result, elections were held in May 2022 for the two new councils now being called Cumberland Council and Westmoreland and Furness Council who would take over local government responsibilities in Cumbria in May 2023. In Westmorland and Furness Council the Liberal Democrats won a majority. In Cumberland, Labour won the election with a large majority. What is also of note is that the number of councillors in Cumbria was reduced by almost two-thirds from almost 330 to 111. However, the overall workload involved in representing local communities, case work, policy development and holding an administrative machine and political leadership will not reduce significantly. It will be much harder for the councillors in the two new authorities, who face a greatly increased workload, but with little prospect of additional resources or support to undertake that work.

In the process, not only have we lost a large number of councillors; we have also lost two important geographical settlements with strong community identities and long civic traditions—the city of Carlisle and the town of Barrow-in-Furness.

Carlisle and Barrow will join the growing list of towns with strong community identities where the link between that identity and local government has been severed in the name of an unproven belief that community identity is irrelevant in such designations, compared with the unproven benefits of economies of scale of service provision. Like Shrewsbury, Durham, Northampton, Scarborough, Crewe, Macclesfield and many other examples, they have become history as far as local government identity is concerned. But it is not beyond the bounds of possibility that their identity could be restored (without great difficulty), as we argue in Chap. 9.

Conclusion

Our account of local government reorganisation in Cumbria shows how an expedient and opportunistic approach to a long-standing policy of creating large unitary councils can play itself out in specific areas of the country. It has also shown how the process starts from a central preference for a larger unitary council to replace a two-tier system with the lower tiered often centred around areas with clear and historical local loyalties and public affinity. It is as though the local in local government is no longer a requirement.

The Cumbria reorganisation taken together with the evidence in the Northamptonshire case study (see Chap. 5) and the 'botched business' which characterised the 2006–08 initiative (see Chap. 4) provide ample evidence that central government and, in particular, the department with oversight of local government are not interested in a balanced evidence-based appraisal of the pros and cons of different structural alternatives. On the basis of recent trends, it seems likely that further opportunities for large unitary authorities will be sought (West Worcestershire? North-East Essex? Mid-Kent?). It is time that a halt was called to this insidious process of undermining the 'local' in local government.

References

Department of Levelling Up, Housing and Communities (DLUHC). (2022). *Levelling up the United Kingdom*. Cmd 604.

Henham Strategy. (2020). *Making counties count: Weaving a new tapestry for local government*.

CHAPTER 7

What Is the Problem About Two-Tier Local Government?

Abstract The two main criticisms of two-tier local government are that it is confusing to the public, who may not understand the division of functions between a county and district; and that it results in an overlap and duplication between the two tiers. Any such confusion is negligible, compared with difficulties the public may have in understanding the division of responsibilities among the large number of public sector organisations who operate in any given area. Overlap and duplication can be seen in positive terms, as providing mechanisms for the expression of different political views—local and strategic—about a particular issue or policy and an opportunity for debate and resolution. Two- or in some cases three-tier systems of local government are to be found in almost all European countries (and in the USA), where they are not seen as problematical. The unitary obsession and the preference for large conglomerate local authorities are peculiar to Britain and is still being played out across England.

Keywords Two-tier local government • Local government size • Local government efficiency • Inter-municipal cooperation • Subsidiarity • Joint working/collaboration • Combined authority • Regions • Devolution

S. Leach, C. Copus, *The Strange Demise of the Local in Local Government*, Palgrave Studies in Sub-National Governance, https://doi.org/10.1007/978-3-031-32819-0_7

Introduction

The case for the creation of unitary councils is founded on a set of assumptions about the shortcomings of a two-tier system. These assumptions are rarely adequately explained or justified by those that deploy them. Their proponents maintain that the two-tier system is confusing to the public and causes duplication and overlap in the provision of public services and the exercise of local government functions. In this chapter we examine respectively the arguments about confusion and overlap and duplication put forward by advocates of unitary councils and highlight their weaknesses. We go on to demonstrate the strengths of multi-tiered local government and explain why it provides for a much more flexible and responsive system than one based on unitary councils, although it is acknowledged that in certain circumstances, unitary authorities are an appropriate structure. The arguments about financial savings, which are also used to justify the creation of unitary councils, are examined in the next chapter.

The Real Source of Confusion

County councils and district councils (and parish councils, where they exist) are but two (or three) of the many public organisations that have service provision and functional responsibilities in any given territory. The profusion of agencies and organisations that deliver public services, spend public money and take decisions that affect the well-being of communities does indeed constitute a complex and opaque patchwork. The Association of Public Sector Excellence (2018:14–15) identified some of the organisations with which local government and the public have to interact. They include, amongst several others:

Police and crime commissioners and authorities
Local enterprise partnerships
National park authorities
Health commissioning bodies
The NHS in all its manifestations from hospital trusts to GP partnerships
Combined authorities
Passenger transport authorities
The probation service
Job centre plus

Various government departments which operate within localities
Fire and rescue authorities
Arm's Length Management Organisations (ALMOs)
Social housing landlords
Academy schools
Various government agencies with service or regulatory responsibilities (including private companies to whom service provision has been contracted out)

These are just some of the organisations and agencies which operate within a fractured and complex network of bodies which the public (and local government) has to navigate. To add to the confusion, these organisations often cover areas which are not co-terminous with those of local authorities or with one another. It is this complex network of public sector organisations which generates public confusion, rather than the division of responsibilities between counties and districts. Indeed, the wider nature of this public confusion is acknowledged in 'Making Counties Count (2020:15–19) and is also something the Levelling Up White Paper accepts (DLUHC, 2022:318). However, like the CCN, the white paper opts for the simplistic solution of merging councils, as a way of solving confusion caused by the proliferation of agencies in the field of service delivery and governance.

In these circumstances to merge the responsibilities of county and district councils into a single body would make at most a marginal contribution to allaying this confusion, which extends far beyond the structure of local government. Indeed, a two-tier system of local government is one of the easiest parts of the network of public provision for the public to comprehend and navigate. Given the growth and widespread use of internet and social media facilities, is it not a relatively straightforward process for citizens to locate information as to which council is responsible for which service? A single phone call can identify whether it is the county or the district which is responsible. 'Who does what' is not something which interests the public on a day-to-day basis and when the need arises it is relatively easy to find who is responsible; far easier, in fact, than navigating one's way through the wider, more complex network of local service providers. Any confusion experienced by the public at the time of the Banham Commission did not prevent them from expressing an overwhelming preference for the continuation of the existing two-tier system, when faced with the alternative of unitary alternatives (a choice confirmed since in the results of local referenda on changing to a unitary system) (see Chap. 8). It is true that there are those—members and officers—who focus on and draw attention to tensions within the two-tier system, usually for political or personal reasons. But such tensions are the exception rather than the rule. Indeed, as illustrated by the District Council All Party Parliamentary Group (APPG) study, there are many and varied examples of effective and co-operative working between county and district councils that show how well the tiered system can and does operate (DCN, 2017). More details are provided in the next section.

Overlap and Duplication

Overlap and duplication are held, by the proponents of large unitary councils, to be 'problems'. But, it is possible to see them in more positive terms. Where so-called overlap and duplication do exist, it is typically because there is a legitimate interest of both counties and districts in the issue concerned (e.g. the location of land allocated for housing, contentious planning issues, economic development priorities). It is healthy from a democratic perspective to have any resulting differences of view exposed and aired in public. In the recent case of the application for a new coal mine in west Cumbria, by the time the application was called in by the government, a difference of view had emerged between Copeland District Council (supportive, on account of the local employment that would be created) and the Cumbria County Council (increasingly concerned by its incompatibility with the strategic challenge of dealing with climate change). Such issues reflect different and legitimate political concerns, which can best be resolved by open and public debate. If there were to be a move to a comprehensive unitary system such legitimate differences between the strategic and the local would be less likely to emerge in the public sphere. Indeed, the larger the local government units become, the less able they are to identify, let alone take account of, differing opinions.

It is also the case that there is considerable scope for dealing with the so-called overlap and duplication, as recent studies of collaboration between councils have demonstrated. Indeed, in his October 2020 ministerial statement, Robert Jenrick has himself acknowledged this potential. His October 2020 ministerial statement noted that restructuring is only one way of the different ways that councils can streamline and make savings; 'joint working with other councils and partners could be an appropriate and sustainable way forward'. Joint working between councils is a long-standing and commonplace feature elsewhere in Europe and a viable alternative to council mergers (see, Hulst & Montfort, 2007; Teles, 2016; Giacomini et al., 2018) and has recently developed considerable momentum in England.

The evidence collected for the report 'District Council Collaboration and Devolution in England' (DCN, 2017) for the All Party Parliamentary Group for District Councils demonstrates that collaboration is a well-established element of the way in which district councils work to transform public services and reduce costs. Drawing on a wide range of examples of innovative and imaginative initiatives, the report shows that district councils are not constrained by their geographical boundaries when developing collaborative arrangements, which are to be found across a wide range of services at a sub-regional or regional level. The political composition of authorities is not a barrier to forging successful co-operative partnerships between districts. Joint working between councils' activity is fast becoming a vital component of the leadership role of district councils, at both political and managerial levels.

Significant progress has been made by district councils in dealing with other public and private sector organisations in partnership-focused activity despite evidence which showed some reluctance on the part of some external bodies to engage. That reluctance reflects the problem of the diminution of the roles and responsibilities of local government and of its standing in the eyes of other public and private bodies. The report shows that district councils have also made substantial contributions to the devolution agenda, involving collaboration across functional economic areas, resulting in the stimulation of economic growth and regeneration. Again, this is a practice which is widespread across local government in Europe, where joint council working is (in different circumstances) an expectation, a government requirement or a local policy tool (see, Haveri, 2003; Citroni et al., 2013; Bouckaert & Kuhlmann, 2016).

The evidence relating to the potential for savings involved in a move from two-tier to unitary local government is explored in the next chapter. But it is important to stress here that even if this outcome could be demonstrated, the case for going ahead on this basis could and should be challenged by reference to the principle of subsidiarity. If one emphasises this principle, there are powerful counter arguments—why should the new Cumberland Council deal with planning applications specific to Workington? Why should Whitehaven not deal with repairs to local roads in response to local demands, in a situation where Cumberland is rightly responsible for the strategic highways network?

Those who deplore the fact that two-tier systems involve duplication or overlap fail to recognise that different territorial levels of community require different spaces within which to interact, debate and make decisions. What may be criticised as overlap and duplication is often in fact a legitimate mechanism for the resolution of differences that operate at different geographical levels. One large unitary council simply cannot capture or accommodate this democratically vital display of difference within its decision-making in the way that a tiered system can.

International Comparisons

While it is possible to construct a case for the creation of unitary authorities in particular circumstances, notably free-standing cities and large towns (the old 'county borough' idea), such areas cover a much more compact geography than a large county: current examples include York, Bedford, Milton Keynes and Telford and Wrekin. There are several other potential candidates (see Chap. 9). But in almost all cases, counties (on existing boundaries) or part counties are simply not viable candidates for unitary status (see Chap. 8).

There are two further reasons why we should be wary of prematurely dismissing two-tier local government. The first is that everywhere else in Europe (and the USA) the case for retaining it in some form is widely accepted and rarely questioned, not least on the basis of the principle of subsidiarity (see above). Unitary local government is a rarity in all the other countries we would be likely to compare ourselves with. Details of local government structures in Europe and elsewhere are provided below. It is possible that advocates for unitary local government in England could be right and everyone else wrong. But it is unlikely. One is reminded of the joke about the admiring parents at their son's involvement in the army recruits passing out parade. One says to the other: 'Look, everyone's out of step but our Brian!'

Table 7.1 provides details of the different patterns of multi-tier local government which operate internationally and have done so unproblematically for many years, invariably complemented by various forms of joint working. It is worth emphasising the fact that there is nowhere else in Europe where towns and cities the size of Northampton, Carlisle, Barrow and Shrewsbury (to name four recent or pending casualties) would not be represented by local authorities based on their boundaries. It has been argued by supporters of large-scale unitary local government that there is an international move in that direction. The OECD (2016) however, found in a study of 101 nations that a two-tier system is the predominant model of local government, with three tiers operating in several countries. Table 7.1 presents a sample (not an exhaustive list) of tiered sub-national / local government systems.

The other major problem for those who wish to see all the remaining shire counties become unitary authorities (whether wholly or in dismembered form) is that this outcome would not bring about a situation in which England came to be dominated by unitary authorities, as is wrongly assumed by the advocates of unitary counties. Indeed, there is an important sense in which such a process would be 'working against the grain' of a different current feature of local government restructuring. Let us explain why.

Table 7.1 Tiered sub-national/local government systems

Belgium: 10 provinces, 581 municipalities
Canada: 3800 municipalities, 10 provinces, 3 territories, 13 provincial areas
Germany: States, 402 counties, 11,902 municipalities, 295 rural districts and 107 district free cities
Spain: 50 provincial councils, 8000 municipalities
Sweden: 21 counties, 290 municipalities
Norway: 11 counties, 356 municipalities (3 municipalities are divided into boroughs)
Denmark: 98 municipalities (5 regions)
Poland: 2477 municipalities, 380 counties, 16 regions
France: 18 regions, 101 departments, approx 2000 cantons, 332 arrondissements, approx 36,000 communes
Italy: 20 regions, 107 provinces and just over 8000 municipalities
Japan: 20 self-governing cities which are independent of the larger jurisdictions within which they are located (much like county and district councils as a parallel) • 42 core cities, 40 special cities • 688 other cities • 745 self-governing towns outside the cities as well as precincts of urban wards • 183 villages
Switzerland: 26 cantons, 2500 municipalities
The US: • most States have two tiers of local government: counties and municipalities • counties may also include townships • municipalities vary between cities, towns, boroughs and villages and the types and nature of these municipalities vary between states

Source: Copus et al. (2020)

In 'Making Counties Count', it is stated that there is a total of 126 single-tier authorities in England, 12 of which are unitary counties or part counties. This is a misconception. There are in fact only 55 unitary authorities, including those recently established in Northamptonshire and Dorset. The report appears to have included in its calculation the 32 London Borough Councils, the 36 Metropolitan District Councils and the councils operating in the Combined Authorities outside the six metropolitan areas (Tees Valley, West of England, Peterborough/Cambridgeshire).

But in Greater London, there is a directly elected mayor and an elected assembly, which clearly constitutes an upper tier within which the London boroughs nest. In the six former metropolitan county areas (and the three additional areas mentioned above), Combined Authorities have been established comprising the leaders of all the constituent councils and headed by a directly elected mayor. If any kind of local election is involved, then the body concerned becomes a local authority, rather than a joint board, which would be the case if there were no elected mayor. Two-tier local government operates in all the Combined Authority areas. Northumberland is not a unitary authority; nor is County Durham. Indeed, even if elected mayors were not involved, the fact that there would exist a city region-wide authority with its own budget would constitute a de facto two-tier system.

At present, some 80% of England's population lives in areas in which a two-tier local government system operates (Copus et al., 2020:16) and doesn't seem too unhappy about the situation (see evidence from the Banham Commission and subsequent public opinion surveys in Somerset and elsewhere). If unitary local government were to be introduced in all counties whose future is yet to be decided, then that figure would rise to 50%, a proportion which would increase if, as seems not unlikely, further combined authorities were to be introduced. Unitary authorities do not dominate the local government map of England and would not do so whatever the outcome of the current partial and piecemeal review.

Conclusion

In this chapter, we have sought to demonstrate that the familiar CCN argument about the two-tier local government system in England being 'past its sell-by date' is misconceived and unviable. A two-tier system has many potential benefits, including its embodiment of the principle of subsidiarity and its capacity for retaining a governmental capacity for settlements with a strong degree of community identity. A tiered system has the advantage of exposing genuine differences of view between the strategic and local levels and a mechanism for resolving such differences, in a way which would be much more difficult in a county-sized unitary authority. Few countries share the view that large unitary authorities provide a satisfactory alternative. And even if this option were to be introduced in all the remaining shire counties, two-tier local government would continue to be experienced by over half of England's population. A pause and a reassessment of the justification for the drift to large unitary authorities are long overdue.

References

Association of Public Sector Excellence. (2018). *Bringing order to chaos: How does local government hold to account agencies delivering public services?*

Bouckaert, G., & Kuhlmann, S. (2016). Comparing local public sector reforms: Institutional policies in context. In S. Kuhlmann & G. Bouckaert (Eds.), *Local public sector reforms: National trajectories and international comparisons* (pp. 1–20). Palgrave Macmillan.

Citroni, G., Lippi, A., & Profeti, S. (2013). Remapping the state: Inter-municipal cooperation through corporatisation and public private governance structures. *Local Government Studies, 39*(2), 208–234.

Copus, C., Leach, S., & Jones, A. (2020). *Bigger is not better: The evidenced case for keeping 'local' government.* District Council's Network report.

Department of Levelling Up, Housing and Communities (DLUHC). (2022). *Levelling up the United Kingdom.* White Paper, London.

District Council Network. (2017). *District council collaboration and devolution in England.*

Giacomini, D., Sancino, A., & Simonetto, A. (2018). The introduction of mandatory inter-municipal cooperation in small municipalities: Preliminary lessons from Italy. *International Journal of Public Sector Management, 31*(3), 331–346.

Henham Strategy. (2020). *Making counties count: Weaving a new tapestry for local government.*

Haveri, A. (2003). Intermunicipal cooperation as a part of local governance. *Finnish Local Government Studies, 31*, 316–325.

Hulst, R., & Montfort, A. V. (2007). Inter-municipal cooperation: A widespread phenomenon. In R. Hulst & A. V. Montfort (Eds.), *Inter-municipal cooperation in Europe.* Springer.

OECD, & United Cities and Local Government (UCLG). (2016). *Subnational governments around the world Structure and finance: A first contribution to the Global Observatory on Local Finances.*

Teles, F. (2016). *Local governance and inter-municipal co-operation.* Palgrave Macmillan.

CHAPTER 8

Why Bigger Is Not Better

Abstract On the basis of a review of over 300 pieces of research evidence it can be demonstrated that the relationship between authority size and performance (efficiency and effectiveness) is unproven; the evidence is inconclusive. On the other hand, the evidence shows that there is a clear relationship between size of authority and the quality of local democracy (as measured by electoral turnout, accessibility of councillors and many other criteria): as size increases so the quality of local democracy deteriorates. The case for large county-based unitary authorities in England is further undermined by a recognition of its incompatibility with community identity, public preference and the fact that most counties in England do not comprise areas which have viability as foci for economic development. If the agenda of the 2020 reorganisation had been taken forward, the disparity between average local authority size in England and in Europe, already substantial, would become even greater and lead to a situation where the term 'local' could no longer meaningfully be applied to sub-national government in England.

Keywords Local government economies of scale • Diseconomies of scale • Local government size • Local democracy • Local government performance • Councillors • Councillor workloads • Combined authority • Regions • Devolution • Community identity

S. Leach, C. Copus, *The Strange Demise of the Local in Local Government*, Palgrave Studies in Sub-National Governance,
https://doi.org/10.1007/978-3-031-32819-0_8

Introduction

There are four principal justifications put forward for large unitary authorities by their advocates. These justifications are repeated in the various reports commissioned and financed by the CCN. The first is the familiar 'economies of scale' argument, complete with predictions provided by consultancy firms such as Price Waterhouse and Ernst Young of the financial savings that could be made by moving to unitary authorities. The larger the unitary authority, the greater the level of savings predicted; the issue of diseconomies of scale is not addressed and no 'maximum size' constraint identified. The content of these forecasts is familiar from county-commissioned input into previous reorganisation initiatives (Banham, the 2006–08 'bidding system'). One fundamental flaw in this approach is that it has invariably been assumed that local authorities are no more than 'service delivery' (as opposed to governmental) agencies. Another is that no attention is paid to the adverse consequences of large unitary authorities for the health of local democracy. The other three justifications relate specifically to the case for unitary authorities based on existing county boundaries and are given most emphasis in the Henman Strategy report 'Making Counties Count'. They comprise the following:

- county-based unitary authorities provide the most appropriate basis for economic regeneration and 'levelling up'.
- local-level input in such authorities can be provided by town and parish councils with enhanced powers or by area committees/panels (or similar devices).
- counties have a historical and cultural resonance in the hearts and minds of residents, which gives them real meaning as local authorities.

In this chapter, we expose each of these justifications to evidence from independent, international academic research and to critical scrutiny, including comparisons with attitudes to local authority size in our European neighbours. We then move on to a wider assessment of the damage that would be caused to the very concept of LOCAL government by a move in this direction.

The next section critically evaluates the value of the current search for an optimal size for local government units and examines the wide range of evidence on the relationship between local authority size and performance.

Section three examines the relationship between size and democratic viability from a similar evidence-based perspective. Section four critically evaluates the case for unitary councils based on English counties.

The Relationship Between Size and Performance

The appropriate size of local authorities and the relationship between size, performance and local democracy have been the subject of considerable independent academic research over the past 30 years. Some 300 pieces of that research were explored for a recent study of these topics (Copus et al., 2020). In this chapter, we provide a summary of the main conclusions which emerge from this comprehensive review and draw on the report, and the evidence it contains, to substantiate our arguments. The findings of the report regarding the size of local government can be crystallised into the following two conclusions (Figs. 8.1 and 8.2).

As a starting point, it should be recognised that England and the rest of the UK for that matter, already stands out from other European countries (and the USA) in its establishment of units of local government with a much greater average size than these comparators. It is true that amalgamations have taken place in some European countries in recent years, but the new councils which have been established still have, on average, much smaller populations than our councils (Denters & Rose, 2005; Denters

> Despite the conviction with which the case is made by the County Councils Network, drawing on commissioned reports from consultants, that increases in council size improve efficiency effectiveness and performance, no consistent or conclusive evidence can be found in the literature surveyed to justify this belief.

Fig. 8.1 Efficiency, effectiveness and performance: size doesn't matter

> On this issue, the literature is far more consistent in its findings that increases in the population size and geographical scale of local government units do have a damaging impact on a range of democratic criteria, including electoral turnout, levels of public engagement, contact between citizens and councillors and levels of affinity with the council held by the public.

Fig. 8.2 Local democracy: size does matter

et al., 2014; Ladner et al., 2015). The current trend to move to large unitary authorities in the shire areas will serve only to accentuate this discrepancy. Copus et al. (2020) note that as far back as 2003, Stewart (2003:181) comments that after the 1974 reorganisation in England, the average size of a shire district was over ten times the average size of lower tier authorities in Europe. He points out that:

> The scale of UK local authorities reflected the dominant conception of such authorities as agencies for the provision of services and associated assumptions of sizeism dominant in governance and public administration. It was widely assumed that size was associated with efficiency, despite the reality that investigations have failed to find any clear link between size and efficiency and/or effectiveness.

Since 1974, whilst the academic evidence continues to be inconsistent and inconclusive, the average size of local authorities has increased considerably, as more and more shire districts have been amalgamated into county or sub county-wide units, increasing the disparity with current practice in the rest of Europe (and, indeed, globally).

The credibility of the causal link between authority size and performance has been challenged by George Boyne (1995:221), whose research led to the following conclusion:

> Analyses of local government reorganization have concentrated on a largely spurious link between population size and the efficiency of service provision. There is little point in setting minimum or maximum populations for local units, because it is the scale of output which counts, not the number of local residents. The level of output is likely to vary considerably for a given population, depending in part on the level of need for different services. Even when needs are the same in different areas, the level of output will vary as a result of decisions on service quantity and quality.

Andrews and his colleagues (2006:4–5) concluded on the basis of detailed research that the relationship between size and performance is a complex mosaic: '*sometimes bigger is better, sometimes small is superior and sometimes medium-sized authorities achieve the best results. The evidence suggests that a universal size formula cannot be applied to decisions on reorganisation.*'

Indeed, a whole series of research projects have undermined the idea that bigger local government is always more efficient, effective and cheaper (see, Muzzio & Tompkins, 1989; Keating, 1995; Byrnes & Dollery, 2002; Dollery & Fleming, 2006; Aulich et al., 2011; Denters et al., 2012; Slack & Bird, 2013; Schaap & Karsten, 2015; Erlingsson et al., 2020).

The implication of these, and other studies, is clear. The persistent efforts of DLUHC and its predecessors to identify an 'ideal size' for local authorities are doomed to failure. It can be likened to the search for 'the philosophers' stone'.

Martin (2005) argues that the size of individual councils may be far less important now than it was assumed to be in the past for three reasons: authorities are increasingly commissioning rather than delivering services: new technology is increasing the opportunities for new forms of delivery across boundaries, decreasing the relevance of 'economies of scale' arguments and the increased emphasis on partnership working has opened up new possibilities for authorities to work together. He concludes that:

> What councils require therefore is not amalgamation, but rather greater freedom to achieve economies of scale involving both the commissioning and delivery of services.

Other research has shown that the quality of local leadership (political and managerial), the allocation of powers, the level of devolved autonomy and the nature of financing regimes all have a greater impact on cost reduction, efficiency, effectiveness and performance measures than does council size (see Baldersheim & Rose, 2010; De Ceuninck et al., 2010; Swianiewicz et al., 2017; Copus et al., 2022: to reference but a few).

Attention should be drawn to some misleading information about international comparisons of authority size contained in the report published by Henman Strategy for the CCN. In arguing for a unitary county the size of Kent (population 1.57 million) they claim that 'a population of this size would barely make it into the top ten of French (regional level) Departments', and that 'there would be two German States (or Lander) which would have smaller populations than a unitary Kent' (2020:34). What the report fails to recognise (or perhaps to point out) is that there are three levels of sub-national government in France, with the Department as the top level, with 332 arrondissements, which are further divided into cantons (not to mention the 36,000 communes). In Germany, below State level there are a further two tiers of local government involving 402 counties and over 12,000 municipalities. It is totally fallacious to imply that French Departments or German Lander be seen as a model for 'large unitary authorities' in England, or indeed anywhere else.

Table 8.1 Average representative ratios

Country	*Population millions*	*Number of lower-tier principle councils*	*Average population per council*	*Total cllrs ('000s)*	*Persons per councillor*
France	67	36,500	1800	515	130
Spain	47	8100	5800	65	720
Germany	83	12,013	6900	200	410
Italy	60	8000	7500	100	600
Belgium	11.5	581	19,700	13	880
Sweden	10	290	34,400	46	220
Netherlands	17	390	43,500	10	1700
Denmark	6	98	61,000	5	1200
England	56	315	177,700	17	3300*

Source: Council of Europe Committee on Local and Regional Democracy (CLRD) (2008) and CEMR/Dexia 2010, 2012 and 2013 (figures updated and rounded for ease of presentation)

Table 8.1 sets out comparative evidence on the average size of local authorities in a number of different European countries and related figures for the average population for which councillors in these countries are responsible.

As can be seen from Table 8.1, councillors in England are required to operate with a much higher representative ratio than any other country in Europe. This discrepancy means that there are fewer councillors to deal with the number and variety of constituents' concerns and to maintain effective monitoring and accountability of the administrative machine.

Table 8.2 illustrates the relationships between the number of municipalities, the total number of councillors and the average number of councillors per council.

Table 8.2 emphasises the fact that countries with smaller populations than England often have far more councils and while the average size of the membership of a municipality may be smaller (reflecting the geographic size of the municipality) councillors are able to work more effectively monitoring service performance than in larger councils.

If, as the evidence shows, there is no demonstrable relationship between local authority size and performance, then the second question becomes crucial; what does increase in size mean for the democratic viability of local government.

Table 8.2 The number of municipalities, the total number of councillors and the average number of councillors per council

Country	*Average number of municipal councillors per municipality*	*Number of municipalities*	*Total number of municipal councillors*
Hungary	5	3163	16,841
Chile	6	345	2240
Portugal	7	308	2086
Iceland	7	74	504
Slovakia	7	2911	20,830
Spain	7	8078	59,136
Czech Republic	10	6234	62,137
Italy	11	7794	87,746
Latvia	14	119	1618
France	14	36,756	524,280
Estonia	15	198	2951
Turkey	15	1364	20,538
Slovenia	16	212	3365
Poland	16	2475	39,959
Belgium	22	589	13,072
Denmark	25	98	2442
Norway	25	429	10,785
The Netherlands	27	340	9175
Greece	30	325	9691
Finland	30	320	9674
Ireland	31	31	949
Sweden	44	291	12,763
England	51	331	17,700
Germany	60	402	23,278

Source: OECD (2017), *Making Decentralisation Work in Chile: Towards Stronger Municipalities*, OECD Multi-level Governance Studies, OECD Publishing, Paris

The Relationship Between Size and Local Democracy

The evidence on the relationship between authority size and efficiency/effectiveness has proved inconclusive and inconsistent. Turning to the relationship between size and local democracy, the evidence is much more consistent and conclusive. Over a wide range of key characteristics of local democracy, it is clear that, as councils increase in size, a series of negative outcomes for local democracy can be identified (Denters, 2002; Denters et al., 2014; Zeedan, 2017; Vabo et al., 2021; Swianiewicz et al., 2022).

The last Royal Commission to consider the future structure of local government—Redcliffe-Maud, which reported in 1969, struggled to balance its desire to recommend larger units of local government with its recognition that such units would have a damaging effect on democratic engagement. The evidence submitted to the Commission convinced it that democratic considerations implied an upper size limit and that if councils became too large, councillors would find it difficult (inter alia) to maintain contact with constituents, hold council officials to account and to comprehend the problems of the area and determine priorities and policy decisions.

> Moreover, the bigger the unit, the more doubtful it becomes whether the individual citizen can have any real sense of belonging to it. People should be able to feel that they are included in a particular unit for the purposes of government because they have a common interest in the area … the distance between the people and their authority therefore must not be too great.
> (Report, cm 4040, 1969 para: 275:72)

One wonders what the commission would have made of the prospect of a unitary Kent (population 1.57 million) as advocated by Henman Strategy in its report for the CCN. Or indeed, whether they would consider that the likes of Cheshire East, North Northamptonshire and Mid Bedfordshire would be likely to generate 'a real sense of belonging' in their inhabitants.

The substantial body of evidence which overwhelmingly confirms the detrimental effects of increasing the population size of local authorities on a wide range of indicators of healthy local democracy is available in Copus et al. (2020). The conclusions of a selection of some of the most pertinent studies are provided below.

Studies by Ladner (2002) and Bagliani (2003) show that public interest in local government is greater in smaller authorities, as is the level of public participation. Three reasons are suggested for these findings:

1. the potential influence of individuals on the outcome of elections is greater in smaller constituencies;
2. there is a stronger identification with municipal matters in smaller constituencies and hence higher levels of participation;
3. social cohesion is higher in smaller municipalities with political participation more likely to be seen as a social duty.

In a comprehensive and detailed study, Denters and his colleagues (2014) looked at a number of indicators for assessing the democratic quality of local political systems, including local political interest, local political knowledge, confidence in local politicians, satisfaction with local government performance and local electoral participation. Their findings demolish any notion that a bigger local government might be better for local democracy. Across the full range of democratic indicators identified increased population size was found to have a negative impact.

Studies by Nielsen (1981) and Vakkala and Leinonen (2016) draw conclusions which confirm the importance of embedding notions of community in local government structure. The concept of community is important in any vision of local government that moves beyond considerations of efficient provision of services into the realm of local identity and proactive local self-government. It is argued, rightly in our view, that the pattern of geographical settlements should form the basis of local government structure. Identification with local authorities is much more likely when they are based on identifiable community areas with identifiable boundaries.

These research findings demonstrate unequivocally that increases in the population or geographical size of councils have a damaging effect on the health of local democracy, as measured by a whole range of criteria including participation, electoral turn out and overall citizen satisfaction. In the context of recent reorganisations in England, it is important to provide more detail about the impact of a move of this nature on four indicators of local democratic health or viability: community identity, public opinion, the workload placed on councillors and the need to sustain democratic viability at local level through active political parties.

Community Identity

In all previous local government reorganisations, up to and including Banham, community identity has been seen as a criterion of major importance, at least equal in weight with that of cost-effective service delivery, sometimes more so. Post Banham, 'community identity' has become marginalised, almost to the point of being ignored. It is central to our argument that a major rebalancing initiative is required if we are to avoid the doomsday scenario we set out in Chap. 6.

There are two distinctive ways of characterising community identity, both highly relevant to the evaluation of reorganisation options:

- affective community, which refers to the sense of identity which people feel with a particular spatial area (village, neighbourhood, town, city, county).
- effective community, which refers to the integrated patterns of activity (work, shopping, leisure) and the journey patterns associated with them, which can be identified around major conurbations (Greater London, Merseyside) or free-standing cities and towns (Nottingham, Leicester, Lincoln).

The last wide-ranging attempt to measure affective community identity was carried out by the Banham Commission in 1992–93. The findings have great significance for the current 'bigger is better' misconception. Taking Lincolnshire as an example, 43% of its population identified very strongly with their village or neighbourhood and 34% identified very strongly with the town in which they lived or near to where they lived. Very strong community identity with the county council area, the district council areas and the three former 'parts of Lincolnshire' were much lower, averaging 13%.

Similar findings were reported in a large majority of the counties involved (see Leach, 1998). There is no reason to suppose that this pattern of loyalties has changed significantly over the following 25 years, particularly as most of the counties currently faced with change are relatively traditional in nature (such as Lincolnshire, West Sussex, Worcestershire, Devon). The fact that the larger the spatial area concerned, the lower is the level of community identity makes it impossible to justify a move to large unitary authorities on the grounds of the criterion of affective community.

It is significant that the unitary authorities recommended by Banham and established in 1996 were almost all town or city-based rather than county-based. A responsiveness to the importance of community identity led to the creation of the unitary authorities in the cities of Derby, Nottingham, Leicester and Bristol, as well as many smaller town-based examples such as Middlesbrough, Darlington, Hartlepool, York, Telford and Milton Keynes (not forgetting tiny Rutland, then a mere 33,000 in population). The average size of the unitary authorities created in the wake of Banham was less than 200,000, a far cry from the 300–500,000 range which has recently been endorsed by government ministers. There were no county-based unitary authorities, apart from Herefordshire. This outcome has lessons for the current initiative. There may well be a case for a further set of unitary authorities based on towns and cities, where community identity is strong, within existing counties; but not for the counties themselves or arbitrary divisions thereof (such as Cheshire East and West Northamptonshire).

The importance of effective community was recognised in the introduction of 'combined authorities' from 2015 onwards. Greater Manchester, Merseyside and Tyne and Wear and others all operate as what have been termed 'functional economic areas', that is, areas with integrated patterns of journey to work, shopping and leisure activities, focused on one or more economic hubs. That was the rationale for the creation of the metropolitan county councils in 1974 and the justification for their recent de facto reintroduction. They are all examples of 'effective communities', to which several other candidates not yet designated as combined authorities could be added. In the light of the emphasis being placed on post-Covid economic regeneration, the potential contribution of a wider spread of combined authorities becomes apparent. The challenge will be to integrate the case for local authority units based on 'affective communities' (which would typically be relatively small in scale) with those based on 'effective communities' (which would typically be much larger in spatial and population terms). This challenge is responded to in the final chapter.

Public Opinion

Public opinion rightly played a major part in the way the Banham Commission framed its recommendations. The Commission understandably wanted to be able to demonstrate that there was at least an acceptable level of support for implementing any change from the existing two-tier system to a unitary option which the Commission had identified in its stage one reports. In some counties, the level of support for such a change could indeed be demonstrated. Banham recommended that the counties of Avon, Cleveland and Humberside should be abolished, because he could demonstrate substantial public support for change, even though it meant the disappearance of counties which exhibited a strong 'effective community' identity. Avon and Cleveland are city regions and have been rightly recognised as such in their recent designation as combined authorities (there has always been more dispute as to whether Humberside can be seen as such). Among the other counties, only in Berkshire was a unitary option recommended (six authorities based on the existing districts). In none of the others could a switch from two-tier to a unitary alternative be justified in the basis of public opinion (see Leach, 1998). It was apparent that the retention of the two-tier system was invariably the preferred option, with a unitary authority based on the county the least favoured.

There is little reason to believe that public opinion has changed since the 1990s. Indeed, in the local surveys that have been carried out in connection with counties subjected to recent reorganisations, a similar pattern has emerged. Referenda carried out in three Shropshire districts in 2007 yielded the following results: in South Shropshire a 57% vote against a unitary Shropshire, in Shrewsbury a 70% vote against and in Bridgnorth, 86%. In the same year, the outcome of a county-wide referendum was a 76% vote opposed to a unitary county. In Christchurch, a Dorset district, 84% of the population was opposed to the creation of a Bournemouth/Poole/Christchurch unitary authority. A referendum in Somerset in 2007 saw 82% vote against the creation of a county-wide unitary. Yet, that did not settle the issue. Somerset was targeted again by the government for a unitary council and a second referendum was held in June 2021 but only presented the voters with two options: a single unitary county-based council or the creation of two-unitary councils across the county (retention of the existing system was not placed on the ballot paper by the districts which organised the referendum). Voters supported, by 65%, the two-unitary option; but from April next year, Somerset will become a county-wide unitary despite public opposition.

The pattern is clear: there is no public enthusiasm for large county-based unitary authorities and a marked preference for smaller councils based on real places with which local people identify. The question can legitimately be asked of why unwelcome changes of this nature should be imposed on local populations which do not support them?

The Workload Placed on Councillors

England already has by far the largest average council population size in Europe and by far the greatest average number of residents for which councillors have responsibility. The more citizens a councillor is expected to represent, the greater the implications for their overall workload and the greater demands on the various roles they are expected to carry out, including working with and responding to residents' concerns; partnership working with local businesses and other relevant public and private sector organisations; taking part in the various decision-making and scrutiny processes of the council; and holding officers of the council and those of other public bodies (e.g. health authorities) to account. This would be a demanding portfolio of roles in a large shire district. In a unitary county the size of Cornwall or North Yorkshire, it would become almost impossible to do justice to these expectations and one wonders how councillors have been or will be able to cope without reaching breaking point. What would become well-nigh impossible, if large unitary authorities were to become the norm, is the capacity of councillors to play an effective 'eyes and ears of local community' role, acting as a two-way conduit between the needs and priorities of local residents, whilst reflecting back to them the limits of the possible (particularly in a time of continued austerity).

The level of interest and involvement which people have in local democratic processes is likely to be influenced both by residence in or near a settlement with which there is a strong degree of local identity and by the accessibility of local councillors. Councillors are, for many local residents, the main link with 'the council'. If you have a problem, you call or e-mail your councillor or attend one of his or her surgeries. If your councillor lives locally, in a ward of manageable population size, then he or she is more likely to be able to play a proactive advocacy role on behalf of local residents, as well as a responsive one, using the opinions and views picked up as a valuable source of local intelligence, potentially beneficial to the council. This is local democracy at its best. It would however be much less feasible in a ward of up to 20,000 in population in a unitary Hertfordshire!

Cornwall provides a pertinent example of the impact of a move from two-tier to unitary local government in a rural area dominated by small towns. Cornwall lacks any sizeable towns; the largest settlement is Falmouth (population 22,000), with Bodmin, Redruth, Cambourne, Penzance and St. Austell amongst the best known of the other towns, with marginally lower populations. When there were six district councils in Cornwall, each of these settlements would have been represented by at least half a dozen councillors, which makes feasible a substantial level of grass roots involvement and activism on their part. Now the reality is that such places will be represented by one or at most two or three local councillors, whose ability to operate in this way will have been greatly compromised. A similar outcome is likely in North Yorkshire, which has a similar kind of settlement pattern ('small town' examples include Ripon, Thirsk, Skipton, Whitby and Richmond).

Maintaining Democratic Viability

In a move to large unitary authorities, the resulting greatly increased population per councillor ratios and the increasing difficulties, in these circumstances, of councillors doing justice to both their local representative and policy-making roles (as discussed above) are in themselves serious threats to democratic viability at the local level. But there is another way in which democratic viability would be diluted by such a move.

It has long been the case that party politics has been a dominant presence in local government. A large majority of those standing at local elections have party political affiliations, as have an even higher proportion of those who end up being elected (at the time of writing around 86% of all councillors across England come from one of the three main parties). Decision-making in local authorities is infused with party politics. Furthermore, political parties have a key role in sustaining local democratic practices. All three major parties have a local dimension to their organisation; local parties and constituency parties, which sometimes but by no means always cover the same territory, form key elements in their constitutions, providing a meeting place for councillors, candidates, party activists and local council members and—for one of the parties—the local MP. Constituency parties spring to life in the months preceding a general election, providing 'on the ground' canvassers and voting facilitation processes which can still make a real difference to electoral outcomes. Local parties play a similar role in respect of local elections, whether at county, district or unitary authority levels or for an elected mayor.

The ideal situation for maintaining local political activity of this nature is one where there are relatively frequent local elections and a congruence between a parliamentary constituency and a local authority. When neither of these conditions is met, as in large unitary authorities where elections are held every four years, then the local party machinery tends to atrophy in the long period between elections—there is little for it to do. In contrast, in the many shire districts which are co-terminous (or largely co-terminous) with a parliamentary constituency, local election will take place either every two years (county and district separately) or three years in four, if the district council holds elections in thirds. As a result, there is always an election approaching and the constituency party will not experience the long periods of inactivity referred to above (the same point holds for local parties in metropolitan district councils, where elections are held three years in four). This will have been the situation in Corby, Kettering,

Wellingborough and East Northants before the creation of North Northamptonshire, but not anymore.

An awareness on the part of MPs of the value of an active local party machinery, not prone to long periods of inactivity, is likely to have been a key influence in the opposition of many backbench Conservative MPs to the government's plans to introduce large unitary authorities, which will certainly have influenced Robert Jenrick's change of direction, set out in his letter of October 12, 2021, to Conservative councillors (see Chap. 6).

A key indicator of local democratic viability is of course the level of turnout at local elections. As noted above (Denters et al., 2014; Gendzwill & Kjaer, 2021; Swianiewicz et al., 2022) there is cross-national evidence that turnout tends to be higher in smaller authorities which reflect places with a strong community identity.

County Councils and Economic Regeneration

The consultancy reports commissioned by the CCN have argued that unitary county councils would be in an ideal position to take forward the economic regeneration agenda which forms an integral part of the government's interrelated devolution and local government reorganisation agendas. But this claim is based primarily on size, rather than areal configuration. Counties are big enough to take on this job; districts would be too small.

But even if one were to accept this size-based argument in principle, the reality is that counties, in their current form do not in most cases constitute viable territorial configurations for this activity. Rarely do they coincide with 'functional economic areas' which are the logical building blocks for economic regeneration, as those responsible for launching the 'combined authorities' initiative rightly recognised.

County councils (as opposed to counties) come in various shapes and sizes, as illustrated by the following categorisation:

- polo mint county councils:

These are the areas which remain when a large city-based unitary authority has previously been designated at or close to the centre of the county area. Examples include Leicestershire, Derbyshire, Notts and Warwickshire. The idea of a county area which excludes the big city at its centre proving a viable focus for economic regeneration is just not credible, unless it operates in co-operation with the core city in a combined authority, in which case it no longer qualifies as a unitary authority. Cumbria is a different kind of polo mint council—in its case the hole in the middle is the Lake District National Park Authority, which exercises independent planning and housing powers. Around the National Park are to be found several distinctive functional economic areas focused on Carlisle, Barrow and West Cumbria. What value could have been added to the economic development function, one wonders, by the imposition of a county-wide unitary authority (although the east-west split to be introduced in 2023 is hardly more credible)?

- Rural counties lacking an economic focus:

Examples include Devon, Lincolnshire, Worcestershire and North Yorkshire and East and West Sussex. Norfolk and Suffolk can also be categorised in this way, although they contain small city regions on their southern edges, as can Hampshire, apart from its southern parts, which largely consist of fringe suburbs of the Southampton/Portsmouth city region.

- Counties bordering conurbations:

Much of the area covered by the counties of Surrey and Hertfordshire are commuter country for the Greater London conurbation, which has widened its sphere of influence since its creation in 1965. The same is true of significant areas of Essex and Kent and of parts of Lancashire (Merseyside and Greater Manchester), Staffordshire (West Midlands and the Potteries). In each case the county lacks a viable basis for economic regeneration and indeed a convincing administrative raison d'etre. There are functional economic areas within these counties (e.g. the Medway towns in Kent, the area centred on Thurrock in Essex), but these are now unitary authorities and what remains of the county areas do not constitute functional economic areas and for this reason are not viable economic regeneration entities. In other cases, functional economic areas straddle county boundaries.

The only counties where there is any kind of case for the county in its entirety qualifying as a functional economic area (in each case, with reservations) are Somerset (although the public rejected this as a reason to create a large unitary), Cambridgeshire and Leicestershire. But to designate the last of these as a unitary authority would result in the disappearance of Leicester as a city-based authority, which it is something it is unlikely that the government would contemplate (although 'Making Counties Count' certainly takes this option seriously). If one is seeking to identify areas best equipped to undertake economic regeneration, then an extension of the 'combined authorities' initiative provides a much more appropriate model than do existing county council areas (see Chap. 9).

County Councils' Capacity for Devolution

County councils, when making bids for unitary status, have often argued that the local dimension in decision-making can be protected without the need for district councils. 'Making Counties Count' predictably supports this argument by claiming that there are two ways in which large counties can introduce accountability at the local level, indeed at a more local level than that of district councils. They can introduce mechanisms such as Local Area Boards or Area Action Partnerships which provide local forums through which the unitary county can be responsive to needs expressed by local residents. Or they can facilitate the spread of town and parish councils in their areas and devolve further powers to them.

The report puts forward two examples of 'good practice' regarding the former—the Area Action Partnerships in County Durham and the Local Area Boards in Wiltshire (Henham Strategy, 2020, pp 32–3). The Wiltshire example claims to 'bring decision-making into the heart of the community'. The Boards 'meet regularly and give people a chance to talk to county council staff and councillors'. But the only powers delegated to them are grants to community groups and 'youth funding in partnership with local youth networks'. In no meaningful sense can this be seen as serious devolution, involving genuine local accountability. Most town councils would carry out a much greater range of functions. The terms 'talking shop' and 'tokenism' spring to mind, as is the case with the Durham example.

And what of the second claim—that the strengthening of town and parish councils can provide a viable local counterbalance to a large unitary county? The problem here is that most of the 9000 town and parish councils across England do not wish to be strengthened and to carry out more functions than they already have. Commenting on local planning applications is the main interest for many of them. Although such councils constitute a valuable grass roots element to our local government system, they vary greatly in their size, capacity, staffing and the nature of the areas they cover. In a recent exercise carried out by one of the authors in a unitary authority of 200,000 population with 29 town and parish councils, four (all town councils) could be defined as active, with responsibility for a reasonably wide range of functions and a sizeable budget. Another half dozen exercised a more limited range of functions and were more modest in their ambitions. The remainder had what can only be described as a minimal role, in several cases meeting only once a year ('the parish meeting'). Experience from elsewhere suggests that this pattern is not untypical. Cheshire East (population 360,000) has 144 town and parish councils which vary greatly in their responsibilities and ambitions.

There is an intriguing contradiction in the county argument that district councils should be abolished, but town and parish councils should be empowered and their coverage extended. Is this not an implicit recognition that large and remote unitary counties would indeed be 'too big', from a democratic and localist perspective, and would need to seek to overcome this problem by reinventing a messier, piecemeal version of the very two-tier system they would like to see abolished?

The same contradiction is apparent when considering Local Area Boards and the like. The less genuine devolution takes place, the more the initiative represents little more than tokenism. The more devolution takes place, the more it involves the replacement of one two-tier system with another; a tacit acknowledgement of the need for such a system in large county areas. The larger the unitary county the more Area Boards would be needed; a unitary Hertfordshire would require around 50 (using a maximum population figure of 20,000; anything higher would not merit the label 'local'). The management of such a complex system would involve a formidable administrative cost. Similar costs and complexity would be involved for any county seeking to extend and empower the range of town and parish councils in its area.

Counties as the Natural Units for Local Government

'Making Counties Count' (2020:7) waxes lyrical about counties as some form of natural unit of government. 'The public understands what a county is and can easily identify with it' it claims. 'Counties have existed for centuries (indeed, as what we call counties are originally Anglo-Saxon units of government), and they have played a key role in shaping our sense of place, our culture and our geographic understanding of ourselves. They provide reference points, they give names to clubs and societies, to sporting teams, dialects and culinary fayre (sic), local traditions and much more. In essence counties are places in the minds of the English people—places where people live and come from, places where they "belong".' The conclusion we are asked to draw is that counties provide such obvious local government units because they are much more than local government units.

What this rosy picture fails to recognise (or perhaps acknowledge) is that all these attributes apply equally, if not more so, to towns and cities, which have the added advantage of generating a much stronger sense of identity and attachment for their local residents than do counties as the MORI research carried out for the Banham Commission clearly demonstrated. The main 'sporting teams' attached to counties are county cricket clubs (which include one deceased county (Middlesex) and several where the county ground is outside the current boundaries of the county (Warwickshire, Lancashire, Hampshire)). Much more potent symbols of local attachment are the football teams representing towns within counties, which attract much higher attendances (Burnley, Preston, Norwich, Ipswich, Oxford and Cheltenham, to name but a few). If local government units are to be based on places with a strong community identity, as it is right that they should, then districts are a much more appropriate starting point than are counties. This comparison serves to highlight what would be lost if all the above towns and cities were to disappear from the local government map, subsumed within a less cherished, more remote county or (just as likely) a sub-division which is neither county- nor town-based. There are several precedents including North Northamptonshire and Cheshire East; are we soon to have imposed on us the likes of Norfolk South, Lancashire East and Hertfordshire West?

The Question of Size: How Big Do You Go?

For advocates of large unitary authorities there are two different interpretations of what 'large' means. In 'Making Counties Count', the preferred unitary option is that they should all be based on existing counties, five of which are over one million in population. Size is no object. 300,000? 1.5 million? No problem—the bigger the better. That would clearly be a view supported by the County Councils Network, the report's clients.

But the interpretation which has developed within DCHLG is different. Ever since they responded to the 2006 bidding system, the preference has been for unitary authorities which are 'large but not too large'. Opportunities to go for a unitary Cheshire (680,000) or even Bedfordshire (400,000) were not taken. The Ministry seemed more at ease then and in the 2015–20 period with unitaries in the 300,000–500,000 range, the only exception being Cornwall (524,000). It has been shown (see Chap. 6) that within DCHLG (and now DLUHC), that there is a belief that there is an ideal size for a unitary authority, if only it could be identified, a belief which might reflect an awareness that, at some population level, diseconomies of scale set in. The fact that a succession of newly appointed ministers have come out with statements which express approval for the above range (see Chap. 3) supports our view. Following our comprehensive review of the literature, we could not find a shred of evidence for an 'ideal size' (see Copus et al., 2020 for a comprehensive review).

But if that is part of the assumptive world of the DLUHC, it is unlikely to be readily jettisoned. In our view, if unitary authorities are to be introduced in all remaining two-tier shire counties (which we sincerely hope is not the case), they are more likely to comprise a bundle of 'part counties' with populations in the familiar DLUHC range, which is not good news for the CCN, nor for the majority of county councils which have populations of 500,000 or over.

There are two potential size-related problems for the advocates of large unitary authorities, whichever interpretation of the term 'large' were to be adopted. There has been an expectation that the introduction of unitary authorities in all the remaining shire counties would in some way simplify local government structure in England, introducing a greater level of consistency. But as we have pointed out (see Chap. 7), even if this were the outcome of the review, two-tier local government would remain the reality for 50% of the country's population. Not much evidence of a move to simplicity and consistency here!

An additional problem for the 'large unitary' enthusiasts is the wide discrepancy in size which would become apparent across the country. Because the main argument for unitary authorities is one premised on economies of scale, then 'large' unitary authorities are much to be preferred to 'small' examples of the genre. As we have shown, there is no consistent independent international research finding that shows this to be a guaranteed outcome (see Keating, 1995; Blom-Hansen et al., 2016; Baldersheim & Rose, 2021). But the average population size of the 55 existing unitary authorities is well below the range (300–500,000) which has been recommended by government over the past few years. Prior to the introduction of the nine new unitary authorities in 2006, the average size of the 46 unitary authorities existing outside the metropolitan areas was under 180,000. Following their introduction, the average figure rose to around 200,000. There are two such authorities with populations of less than 100,000 (including Rutland at 45,000) and 23 with populations in the range 100–200,000. If a unitary Hartlepool (93,000) and Darlington (103,000) are viable entities, how is that compatible with the DCHLG preferred range of 300–500,000, let alone the scenario which includes five unitary counties with populations of over one million? The local government map of England would remain akin to a dogs' breakfast.

Conclusion

Those who argue for large unitary authorities (300–500,000 or above) do so almost exclusively on cost efficiency grounds; the claim that such authorities will cut costs and save money. The evidence they provide comes predominantly from consultancy firms, who provide detailed forecasts of the savings that they consider could be made under such a scenario, typically suggesting that the larger the unitary authority concerned the greater the level of savings that could be achieved. There is no acknowledgement of the impact of diseconomies of scale which economists have suggested would be likely to have a significant countervailing impact, particularly as one moves up the population ladder into the realm of a unitary Kent (population over 1.5 million).

There is no argument made that the quality of services (however measured) would be any better in large unitary authorities, only that they could be provided more cheaply. The one exception is the claim that 'strategic services' need a level of population in the above range if they are to prove effective. But by far the most common conceptions of 'strategic services' are those associated with planning of land-use, highways, public transportation and economic development within city regions or 'functional economic areas', as identified in most (but not all) of the designation of the post 2015 Combined Authorities in the former metropolitan counties and elsewhere. Size itself is not a relevant consideration. As we have argued, in no sense could the county areas of Hertfordshire or Warwickshire (or many others) be seen as appropriate locations for strategic planning of this nature.

As we have argued earlier in this chapter, a comprehensive cross-national review of the evidence for the economies of scale claimed by the advocates of large unitary authorities is inconclusive. But even if it wasn't, it would not in itself provide a justification for a move in that direction. As we noted in Chap. 3, in all local government reorganisations over the past hundred years, up to and including that of the Banham and Cooksey Commissions, arguments about possible economies of scale have been required to be set against arguments about community identity (and, in many cases community preference). As we have seen in this chapter, the implications of what we know about community identity leads to a conclusion of 'the smaller the better' rather than the 'larger the better'. And across a whole range of indicators of democratic health, the comprehensive cross-national review of the evidence shows that large unitary authorities perform worse than smaller unitaries, two-tier systems or indeed any conceivable alternative.

If local government was concerned solely with providing or commissioning services at the lowest possible cost to the council taxpayer, then although the case for large unitary authorities would not be proven, it would have to be taken seriously. But local government has never been restricted to service provision; the term 'government' implies much more than this. In the Lyons report of 1997, the term 'place-shaping' was coined. This is what local authorities have always done; they have 'shaped the places' they represent, not just by providing services, but by developing some form of long-term vision (or strategy, or whatever they choose to call it) for the areas they represent, covering broader economic, social and environmental goals and using a variety of means to achieve them.

But for the term 'place-shaping' to have any real meaning, it should surely refer to places which have real meaning for their inhabitants. Wellingborough, Kettering and Corby are real places with strong community identities; North Northamptonshire is a conglomerate with little community resonance. Barrow and Carlisle are real places, which is not true of the proposed unitary authorities in East and West Cumbria.

As the following chapter makes clear, we are not against unitary authorities per se; there are situations where they are arguably the most appropriate form of local government. Nor are we unqualified supporters of the status quo in the existing two-tier counties. There are several district councils which would be likely to fail the community identity test (their names are often the giveaway—Wyre, Waveney, Waverley). But what we are clear about is that if England were to end up with an across-the-board structure of large unitary authorities, it would be the end of LOCAL government as we know it and the biggest act of civic vandalism in the history of this venerable institution.

Henman Strategy in 'Making Counties Count' states that 'we feel so strongly about the merits of unitary authorities that we think the government should consider insisting on unitary councils across the whole of the country' (p. 40). Well, it may be the dream of Henman Strategy, of Michael Heseltine (2012: 203), who has advocated that all two-tier areas should move to a unitary, and of those in DLUHC seeking a life of greater administrative convenience. But to us it is a nightmare scenario. A unitary Kent with a population of over 1.5 million (three times greater than the state of Wyoming in the USA)? No thank you. Don't vote for R.E Mote!

References

Andrews, R., Boyne, G., Chen, A., & Martin, S. (2006). *Population size and local authority performance: Final research report.* Department of Communities and Local Government.

Aulich, C., Gibbs, M., Gooding, A., McKinley, P., Pillora, S., & Sansom, G. (2011). *Consolidation in local government: A fresh look.* Australia Centre for Local Government Excellence, Local Government Association of South Australia, Local Government New Zealand.

Baglioni, S. (2003). *The Effects of political institutions and city size on political participation: The Swiss case.* Paper presented to ECPR Joint Sessions, Edinburgh, 28th March–2nd April, 2003.

Baldersheim, H., & Rose, L. (2021). Consequences of forced municipal mergers: Evidence from Norway; Ch 339-62. In M. Lackowska, K. Szmigiel-Rawska, & F. Teles (Eds.), *Local government in Europe: New perspectives and democratic challenges.* Bristol University Press.

Baldersheim, H., & Rose, L. (2010). *Territorial choice: The politics of boundaries and borders.* Macmillan.

Blom-Hansen, J., Houlberg, K., Serritzlew, S., & Treisman, D. (2016). Jurisdiction size and local government policy expenditure: Assessing the effect of municipal amalgamation. *American Political Science Review, 110*(4), 812–831.

Boyne, G. (1995). Population size and economies of scale in local government. *Policy and Politics, 23*(3), 213–222.

Byrnes, J., & Dollery, B. (2002). Local government failure in Australia? An empirical analysis of New South Wales. *Australian Journal of Public Administration, 61*(3), 54–64.

Copus, C., Kerley, R., & Jones, A. (Eds.). (2022). *A modern guide to local and regional politics.* Edward Elgar.

Copus, C., Leach, S., & Jones, A. (2020). *Bigger is not better: The evidenced case for keeping 'local' government.* District Council's Network report.

Council of Europe Committee on Local and Regional Democracy (CLRD). (2008). *Report on the relationship between central and local authorities: Situation 2007.* Council of Europe, Strasbourg, France.

Denters, B. (2002). Size and political trust: Evidence from Denmark, the Netherlands, Norway and the United Kingdom. *Environment and Planning C: Government and Policy, 20*, 793–812.

Denters, B., & Rose, L. (2005). *Comparing local governance: Trends and developments.* Palgrave Macmillan.

Denters, B., Mouritzen, P., & Rose, L. (2012). *Size and local democracy: A summary of findings from Switzerland, Norway, Denmark and the Netherlands.* Conference paper at the 22nd IPSA World Conference, Madrid, Spain, 8–12 July 2012.

Denters, B., Goldsmith, M., Ladner, A., Mouritzen, P. E., & Rose, L. (2014). *Size and local democracy.* Edward Elgar.

De Ceuninck, K., Reynaert, H., Steyvers, K., & Valcke, T. (2010). Municipal amalgamations in the low countries: Same problems, different solutions. *Local Government Studies, 36*(6), 803–822.

Dollery, B., & Fleming, E. (2006). A conceptual note on scale economies, size economies and scope economies in Australian local government. *Urban Policy and Research, 24*(2), 271–282.

Erlingsson, G., Jörgen Ödalen, Ó., & Wångmar, E. (2020). How coerced municipal amalgamations thwart the values of local self-government. *Urban Affairs Review, 57*, 1–26.

Gendzwill, A., & Kjaer, U. (2021). Mind the gap, please! Pinpointing the influence of municipal size on local electoral participation. *Local Government Studies, 47*(1), 11–30.

Heseltine, M. (2012). *No stone unturned in pursuit of growth.* TSO.

Henham Strategy. (2020). *Making counties count: Weaving a new tapestry for local government.*

Keating, M. (1995). Size, efficiency and democracy: Consolidation, fragmentation and public choice. In D. Judge, G. Stoker, & H. Wolman (Eds.), *Theories of urban politics* (pp. 117–134). Sage.

Ladner, A. (2002). Size and direct democracy at the local level: The case of Switzerland. *Environment and Planning C: Government and Policy, 20*(6), 813–828.

Ladner, A., Keuffer, N., & Baldersheim, H. (2015). Final report Tender No 2014. CE.16.BAT.031: Self-rule Index for Local Authorities. European Commission.

Leach, S. (1998). The local government review: A policy perspective. In S. Leach (Ed.), *Local government reorganisation: The review and its aftermath.* Frank Cass.

Martin, S. (2005). *The implications of local devolution for efficiency and effectiveness in service delivery.* Note to the seminar of the Lyons Inquiry into Local Government Funding, 22 June 2005.

Muzzio, D., & Tompkins, T. (1989). On the size of the city council: Finding the mean. *Proceedings of the Academy of Political Science, 37*(3), 83–96.
Nielsen, H. J. (1981). Size and evaluation of government: Danish attitudes towards politics at multiple levels of government. *European Journal of Political Research, 9*(1), 47–60.
Royal Commission on Local Government, Vol. 1 Report, cm 4040, 1969 (Redcliffe-Maud).
Schaap, L., & Karsten, N. (2015). *Evaluating municipal mergers' effects: A review of amalgamation studies in the Netherlands.* Paper presented at the Political Studies Association, Sheffield, March 30–April 1.
Slack, E., & Bird, R. (2013). *Does municipal amalgamation strengthen the financial viability of local government? A Canadian example.* International Center for Public Policy Working Paper 13-05, Georgia State University, Atlanta.
Stewart, J. (2003). *Modernising British local government: An assessment of labour's reform programme.* Palgrave Macmillan.
Swianiewicz, P., Gendzwil, A., & Zardi, A. (2017). *Territorial reforms in Europe: Does size matter?* Territorial Amalgamation Toolkit, Council of Europe Partnership for Good Governance.
Swianiewicz, P., Gendzwill, A., Houlberg, K., & Klausen, J. E. (2022). *Municipal territorial reforms of the 21st century in Europe.* Routledge.
The Council of European Municipalities and Regions (CEMR) and Dexia Credit Local. (2011/2012 edition). *Factsheet, EU subnational governments 2010 key figures.* CEMR and Dexia, Brussels.
The Council of European Municipalities and Regions (CEMR) and Dexia Credit Local. (2012). *Factsheet.* CEMR and Dexia, Brussels.
The Council of European Municipalities and Regions (CEMR) and Dexia Credit Local. (2013). *A figure-based portrait of local and regional Europe.* CEMR and Dexia, Brussels.
Vabo, S., Fimreite, A. L., & Houlberg, K. (2021). Why such a different choice of tools? Analysing recent local government reforms in Denmark and Norway. *Local Government Studies.* https://doi.org/10.1080/03003930.2021.2013210
Vakkala, H., & Leinonen, J. (2016). Current features and developments of local governance in Finland: The changing roles of citizens and municipalities. In U. Sadioglu & K. Dede (Eds.), *Theoretical foundations and discussions on the reformation process in local governments* (Advances in Public Policy and Administration (APPA) Book Series) (pp. 304–328). Information Science Reference, IGI Global.
Zeedan, R. (2017). Bigger but not always better: Size and democracy in Israeli amalgamated local governments. *Journal of Urban Affairs, 39*(5), 711–728.

CHAPTER 9

Where Do We Go from Here?

Abstract It would be possible to reverse the direction of the move to large unitary authorities without the need for a formal commission-based reorganisation, which is unlikely to be seriously considered in the foreseeable future by any form of government. The combined authority model could be extended to other parts of the country (e.g. the Portsmouth/ Southampton city region), wherever appropriate, and its accountability strengthened through direct election. Rural regions could be designated in other parts of the country. An organic process, based on the principle of subsidiarity, could be introduced whereby any pre-1974 county borough, municipal borough or urban district could (subject to a local referendum) reclaim its former status and be allocated responsibilities commensurate with its size and socio-economic nature. In this way, the significance of the 'local' in local government could be reintroduced and the move towards large unitary conglomerate authorities halted and reversed.

Keywords Combined authority • Regions • Subsidiarity • Devolution • Unitary local government • Two-tier local government • Localism • Elected mayors • Local government reorganisation

S. Leach, C. Copus, *The Strange Demise of the Local in Local Government*, Palgrave Studies in Sub-National Governance,
https://doi.org/10.1007/978-3-031-32819-0_9

Introduction

What are the implications of the analysis set out in the preceding chapters for the ways in which England's local government structure might beneficially be changed? In responding to the many inconsistencies apparent in the current structure, it is helpful to distinguish between short-to-medium term and longer-term agendas.

In the longer term, it is conceivable that a government of the day might be persuaded to carry out a fundamental evidence-based review of local government structure, involving a thoroughness last seen in the work of the Redcliffe-Maud Commission of 1969 (and to a lesser extent in that of the Banham Commission (1992–95)). But we could wait a very long time for that. It is important, therefore, to consider what might usefully be done over the next few years. Our argument is that a staged process can be identified which would redress much of the damage done by the centre's ill-considered enthusiasm for large unitary authorities in inappropriate locations.

The next section examines the importance of scrapping any extension of the 'large unitary authority' reorganisation programme and discusses the scope or extending central government's Combined Authorities initiative. It also provides a number of suggestions as to how the 'local' element in English local government can be enhanced. The third section sets out the stages through which this goal could be achieved. The chapter concludes with an explanation of why we believe so passionately that local government could and should indeed, be truly local.

Extending and Democratising the Combined Authority Model

The most important short-term imperative is to call a halt to the 25-year long drift to large unitary authorities. The damage wrought to local democracy, to the capacity of councillors to do a proper job, to the link between community identity and local councils and indeed to the very survival of LOCAL government has already been set out at length in these pages. Robert Jenrick's ministerial statement of October 12, 2020, with its clear message that the government is stepping back from the imposition of top-down Whitehall 'solutions' provided a welcome opportunity to consider other less damaging options, but the uncertainty remains. Maybe the DLUHC team responsible for pushing the unitary agenda at every opportunity could be found work elsewhere and replaced with officials with more open minds.

Our starting point is the 2015 Northern Powerhouse policy initiative, which has in seven metropolitan areas allocated a range of strategic functions—economic development public transport and highways planning to Combined Authorities (CAs) comprising an elected mayor and the leaders of the constituent districts. What this model has in effect done is to reintroduce two-tier local government in the larger provincial metropolitan regions. The big cities of Manchester, Birmingham, Liverpool and Sheffield and indeed all of the existing metropolitan district councils and London Boroughs are no longer unitary authorities. They remain hugely influential, but they are now working within a strategic framework provided by these CAs. It is the presence of an elected mayor which makes them de facto local authorities, rather than joint boards. They are in effect the Greater Manchester, West Midlands, Merseyside and West and South Yorkshire Metropolitan County Councils reborn!

In Tyne and Wear, there are separate 'combined authorities' north and south of the Tyne respectively, clearly a nonsense when it comes to transportation planning. Similar schemes have been initiated in the Bristol area (excluding North Somerset), Tees Valley (including Darlington), Peterborough and Cambridgeshire (a strange choice of location) and Cornwall (an even stranger choice and one where the requirement for an elected mayor has been dropped).

Patchy though progress has been, there is a workable model here, at least for the short-to-medium term. There are other city regions that currently lack an area-wide authority, but where the case for one is in principle just as strong as in the areas where combined authorities have already been designated. The Potteries, the Portsmouth/Southampton area, the Fylde, the Calder Valley towns in Lancashire and Greater Leicester, Derby and Nottingham are all eminently suitable locations for the application of 'Northern Powerhouse' principles. Indeed in August 2022, Derby, Derbyshire, Nottingham and Nottinghamshire councils signed up to a devolution deal which, subject to the progress of the Levelling Up and Regeneration Bill, will see the first mayoral election in May 2024.

The principle of subsidiarity, with the Combined Authorities dealing with the strategic conurbation-wide issues and the districts responsible for those functions more appropriate at a local level, would then become widespread throughout the city regions of England.

But there is a problem about the nature of accountability in the CAs. The form of government which has been introduced is diffuse, with opaque accountability linkages. The only directly elected element is the elected mayor. But in each case, decision-making responsibilities are shared with the leaders of the district councils in the area, who were elected to serve Manchester, Birmingham or Leeds, not Greater Manchester, West Midlands or West Yorkshire. In this sense CAs have a strong element of the 'Joint Board' about them, a model featuring indirect (delegate) democracy rather than the direct version which exists in all other local authorities. Joint Boards were widely (and justifiably) criticised when they were introduced in 1986 to replace the metropolitan county councils. The problem has been overcome in the Greater London Authority, which is directly elected. There is a strong case for replicating this approach in CAs, present and future.

There are three implications which follow from the extension of the CA model. First, the model would clearly be much less appropriate for large tracts of rural England. The Northern Powerhouse initiative was conceived in relation to large metropolitan areas and although, as we have shown, there is considerable scope for extending it further, it would lose its purpose, if, for example, it was to be applied to rural Lincolnshire, most of Devon, East Anglia or the tracts of London suburbia that lie outside the boundaries of the GLA (much of Hertfordshire, Essex and Surrey). Some other form of initiative—perhaps 'rural regional authorities'—would be required in these 'leftover' areas.

Second, the existing counties, once the new combined authorities had been taken out, would not, in many cases, provide an appropriate basis for such rural regions. In cases where they do so, they should be re-designated as such; counties too have a place in the many residents' identities and loyalties, though rarely as strongly as do towns. But many of them would not provide a convincing focus or socio-economic identity, particularly where large towns and cities have been taken out of their purview, as in Lancashire, Nottinghamshire and Leicestershire, or they include significant areas of metropolitan suburbia (e.g. Hertfordshire and Surrey). For the present, the designations and boundaries of the existing districts should be retained, although we will argue that there is a strong case for reviewing the most appropriate scale of these lower tier authorities at a later stage.

Third, an interim restructuring of this nature would provide an opportunity to install (or in some cases reinstate) unitary authorities (on the county borough' model), based on cities or larger towns, where there is a strong case for doing so. The authors should emphasise here that they are not opposed to the idea of unitary authorities per se. In the pre-1974 local government map, there existed 79 unitary authorities. They were called county boroughs. After 1974, all of them ended up ceding powers to metropolitan or county councils, usually with extreme reluctance. In the metropolitan areas this concession was totally justified for the reasons set out in Chap. 3. But outside these areas there were plenty of real places, which, if county boroughs had remained on the agenda, could with good reason have been so specified as such. Several of them did become unitary authorities in 1995, following the reports of the Banham and Cooksey Commissions: Swindon, York, Blackburn with Darwen, Blackpool, Brighton and Hove and Milton Keynes, to name but a few. The 'big cities' outside the metropolitan areas—Leicester, Derby, Nottingham, Stoke-on-Trent and Plymouth—were also delighted to recover their independence from their parent counties, after 20 years of resenting their diminished status.

There is a big difference between unitary authorities based on real places such as York, Swindon and Luton and the newcomers such as Cheshire East, North and West Northamptonshire and Central Bedfordshire. The link between community identity and local government structure would be enhanced rather than diminished, if towns such as Carlisle, Barrow, Norwich, Ipswich and Exeter regained their former unitary status. If this were to occur, there would be more relatively small unitary authorities with populations of 75,000 and above. But there are already many such authorities to be found in Teesside, the former county of Berkshire, and Rutland which operate unproblematically. Community identity should be the basis for such designation, not an arbitrary larger population figure, conjured up in some dark corner of DLUHC.

There is a further complication regarding the boundaries of many of the existing 'big city' unitary authorities within shire counties. The area of influence of Leicester, Nottingham, Derby, Plymouth and others has long extended well beyond their city boundaries. Greater Nottingham includes the district councils of Rushcliffe and Gedling (amongst others); Greater Leicester includes Oadby and Wigston, Blaby and Narborough. All these district councils are at least to some extent suburbs of the adjacent cities. If a key role of unitary authorities outside London and the six former metropolitan county areas is to operate as effective strategic authorities, they need to cover, as far as feasible, wider areas of influence. The same point could be made for Norwich, Ipswich and Oxford, all currently designated as shire districts. There is a precedent for boundary extensions of this nature; in 1996, the City of York's boundaries were extended to enable the creation of a small but viable city region-based authority. But such changes should not be forced on reluctant local citizens.

There is a potential problem here. The spirit of the proposals set out in this chapter is that they should involve, wherever possible, a process of organic boundary changes negotiated between councils, and local citizens via referenda, which is much to be preferred to a centrally imposed abolition or amalgamation of councils. But in a new combined authority (such as the one to be focused on Derby and Nottingham), re-designated as a directly elected upper-tier metropolitan council with an elected mayor, several of the shire districts which border the existing cities are significantly smaller than their counterparts in the former metropolitan counties such as Greater Manchester or the West Midlands. They may not wish to become equivalent most-purpose authorities in their own right, nor may it be appropriate, in cases of small size (e.g. Oadby and Wigston, south of Leicester) for them to do so. The solution should be left to the districts involved and their local citizens to agree if they wish to merge, or to decide upon enhanced joint working arrangements between one another and/or the upper-tier metropolitan council.

Drawing together the threads of this analysis, we can identify six features of the current local government structure of England which require reassessment in an interrelated way, if we are to move towards a structure which has a much stronger element of coherence about it than does the current chaotic pattern:

- The case for extending the Combined Authority model.
- Strengthening the accountability of existing and future Combined Authorities.
- The designation of 'rural regions' in those areas for which the combined authority model would not be appropriate.
- The extension of the boundaries of existing city-based unitary authorities in the shire county areas to encompass their effective areas of influence jointly negotiated with and between district councils and involving local citizens in the decisions and without centrally imposed restructuring.

- An acknowledgement that on a criterion of community identity, unitary authorities can be much smaller than the current 300,000 + yardstick.
- The designation of large free-standing towns in the shire county areas as unitary authorities, where appropriate on extended boundaries.

The benefits of introducing these changes are that they would spread the advantages of two-tier local government to the whole of the country and retain the civic identity of many large towns which would otherwise disappear within a further tranche of unitary counties or part counties. It would reintroduce the principles underlying the 1974 reorganisation, which have been too summarily rejected over the years, and spread the metropolitan version of this system to an additional set of areas where the principles are clearly appropriate. But what would not have been achieved is a more wide-ranging reintroduction of the link between places with a demonstrable community identity and civic history and the definition of local authorities, a link which was severed in many areas by the amalgamation of such 'real places' in the metropolitan and shire areas. It is to this issue which we now turn.

Back to the Future: The Re-localisation of English Local Government

Simon Jenkins, writing in 2004 about the state of local government structure in England (Jenkins 2004, p 106), reminded us of the advantages of the system which operated before the 1974 reorganisation

> The map of local government that existed prior to 1974 was a good one. The map survives in essence to this day and there is no good reason for tearing it up. It accepts two tiers in rural areas of county councils and subsidiary municipalities. This is as it has been for a century past. It reflects local sentiments and loyalties of people nationwide. It has diversity without complexity. It is proven abroad.

Since 2004, much damage has been done. But as a template for the future, his vision remains a powerful one. In our view, there would be much to be gained by exploring the scope for a return to a structure based on the 'local sentiments and loyalties of people nationwide', which correspond to the 'real places' to which we have referred throughout the book. It would reintroduce the principle of subsidiarity—the allocation of governmental responsibilities to the lowest feasible level—into English local government and to encourage a much-needed revitalisation of local democracy. As we will argue, this change could be accomplished in a gradual fashion; there would be no need for a costly 'big bang' reorganisation.

The next step in the rural regions would be to facilitate the re-designation as local authorities of the medium-sized towns which before 1974 operated as municipal boroughs or urban districts. Thus, in Lincolnshire, places like Louth, Skegness and Gainsborough would reappear on the local government map; as, in Hertfordshire, would Hertford, Letchworth and Hitchin, all of them distinctive places which lost their civic identities in 1974. It would be necessary to make a distinction between more populous settlements of this nature (30–70,000) and those with smaller populations (10–30,000) in terms of the level of devolution which was appropriate. For towns with a smaller population (below 10,000) provision should be introduced to take on a wider range of responsibilities than they are currently permitted to operate as 'town councils'. These figures, although they approximate broadly to the relative population sizes of the former municipal boroughs and urban districts, should be regarded as indicative. We would be the last to argue for the imposition of arbitrary population limits regarding qualification for responsibility for local functions. But some kind of guidelines would need to be established.

This 'three-level' of approach would put into operation the principle of subsidiarity—devolution to the lowest feasible level.

The same process should be applied in the succession of shire counties which have been transformed—wholly or partly—into unitary authorities, between 2005 and the present day. It is here, in Cheshire East and West, Northamptonshire North and West, Wiltshire, Shropshire, Durham and others, where the greatest damage has been done to the link between community identity and local government. Where appropriate it may be possible in some cases to retain the counties, re-designated as rural regions, but as part of a two-tier system rather than as unitary authorities.

In the former metropolitan counties, there would also be some scope for strengthening the link between community identity and the definition of local authorities. In Kirklees in West Yorkshire, Huddersfield and its surrounding area could be detached from the towns once specialising in woollen goods such as Dewsbury and Batley, with which Huddersfield has traditionally had little in common. On Merseyside, Southport should once again become a local authority in its own right, as should West Bromwich in the West Midlands and Leigh and its surrounding towns in Greater Manchester. There are many 'real places' across the country that could be reinvigorated in such a way.

But in the cases mentioned above, and the other suitable candidates, such detachments could be introduced with the result of only a small increase in the number of metropolitan districts in the counties affected. If Hartlepool, Darlington, Slough and Wokingham (and indeed Rutland!) are viable authorities, why are not Huddersfield and Southport?

In the existing combined authorities, elected mayors have been seen by the government as an essential part of the deal, although this condition has not always been insisted upon. In most of these areas (and in Greater London), the mayors concerned such as Andy Burnham in Greater Manchester and Andy Street in the West Midlands have developed a high profile and become widely recognised locally and nationally. There is no reason not to continue with this approach in places like South Hampshire, and the Fylde area and the Calder Valley in Lancashire.

Elected mayors have not been adopted in any of the shire county areas, with only the odd exception at district level (Mansfield and Watford). One possibility would be to require that the introduction of elected mayors in such areas be subject to local referenda. The other would be to accept the alternative of mayors being elected from within the rural regional council, rather than in a separate election, although the office holder would lack the direct mandate of an elected mayor, and could be seen to lack the visibility and accountability criteria the government seeks.

There are thus three further inputs to a process of redrawing the local government map of England in a community—sensitive way

- A (limited) redrawing of the boundaries of the metropolitan districts and London boroughs to strengthen the match between community identity and local council definition.
- An opportunity for the devolution to community-based authorities (of a viable local size) which existed prior to 1974 of many of the powers they then enjoyed as municipal boroughs or urban districts.
- An opportunity for smaller towns, currently operating as town councils to acquire enhanced powers (to an appropriate level)

What we would be proposing, if we were in a position of power or influence, would be a phased series of changes which would result in an English local government map which reintroduced the principles of subsidiarity and localism and which rebuilt the links between council definition and local community identity, after a long period in which these links have been progressively dismantled. There is no need for a costly 'big bang' approach to local government reorganisation, which would not be in the spirit of these key values. The various changes to the local government structure should be introduced in a four-stage process, which gradually introduced a model sensitive to the patterns of community and identity which exist and so improve the quality of local democracy and the extent of public participation. We would be tempted to label the process 'organic change' (for that is an accurate description) were it not for the use of this term in Peter Shore's abortive 1978 policy initiative which was in essence a limited one-off politically partisan transfer of powers to cities in shire counties and was in no sense 'organic'!

Stage One:

- Calling a halt to the introduction of large unitary authorities in the shire counties.
- Establishing combined authorities in other city regions and metropolitan areas where this is justified.

Stage Two:

- Establishing 'rural regional councils' in areas not covered by combined authorities, based on existing counties where appropriate and working in conjunction with existing shire districts and parish councils.
- The designation of large, free-standing towns outside the combined authorities as unitary authorities (county boroughs), where appropriate.

Stage Three:

- Reviewing the boundaries of metropolitan districts and London boroughs to move towards a better fit between community identity and authority definition.

- An extension of the boundaries of cities and large towns to encompass suburban areas within their sphere of influence or the establishment of new MDC-equivalent authorities in these areas, with the details and decisions about how to achieve that left to the districts concerned and their local citizens.

Stage Four:

- Providing an opportunity for medium-sized towns (with populations above 10,000) in rural regional authorities to regain the powers they enjoyed (as municipal boroughs or urban districts) prior to 1974, where there is demonstrable public support for this outcome)
- Providing a similar a similar opportunity for small towns (with populations below 10,000), currently operating as town councils, to take on enhanced powers appropriate to their size.

The authors are well aware that these proposals would be likely to be regarded as heresy in the corridors of Whitehall. For those in the DLUHC, the Treasury and elsewhere who have the technocratic, service delivery model of local government embedded in their mind-sets, they would seem ridiculous, because notions of place-shaping, community identity and local democracy have rarely been seen by them as remotely relevant to questions of local government structure. Unworkable, costly, reinventing history, 'pie-in-the-sky' are among the reactions we are anticipating, as our vision challenges the conventional wisdom that 'bigger is better'. Others more supportive of more localised local government would wonder why we were advocating such changes at a time when local authorities are struggling to provide basic services after a long period of resource famine. Their plight is something which we readily acknowledge. But it should not be seen as an obstacle to reminding ourselves about what purpose local government is ultimately meant to serve and to lift our eyes and minds to a time when such changes prove feasible. We have no doubts about their desirability.

It is crucial to approach the issue of local government reorganisation with a fresh perspective and timely to reassess the value of smaller-scale structural features that have served us (and the rest of Europe) well in the past. For over 30 years, the approach to local government structure has been dominated by a drift to large unitary authorities (local government reorganisation by stealth), which have increasingly introduced 'non-places' or convenient lines on a map. This has become the unchallenged conventional wisdom. Local government is too important a feature of our democratic world to be treated in this way. It is time for a radical rethink, before the remaining counties are carved up into the likes of East West Sussex, North Suffolk and West Essex and its structure becomes unique in Europe, for all the wrong reasons.

But let us assume that our arguments to prevent this outcome fall on deaf ears and the doomsday scenario depicted in Chap. 6 comes to pass. That need not be the end of the story; indeed, given the plethora of reorganisations over the last 50 years, it would be premature to expect this to be the case. Let us further assume (a big assumption we admit) that a government eventually comes to power with a recognition that the pattern of large unitary authorities in the shire areas which had been created by its predecessor does not constitute LOCAL government in any meaningful sense of the term and wishes to resurrect the connection between places with which local people have a strong identity and local government units based on these places. There would in principle be a relatively straightforward way of achieving this goal. Most real places that lost their local government identity in 1974 have established town councils.

It is highly likely that in all the real places which have been submerged in meaningless conglomerates like West Northamptonshire will similarly choose to establish town councils, as is their legal right. Northampton, with a population of over 200,000, has already done so, making it the most populous town council in England. Legislation could easily be introduced which enabled any town council above a specified size to reclaim responsibility for those services which it lost as a result of the move to large unitary authorities, as discussed in *Stage Four* of our recommended process of change. Indeed, this provision could and should be extended to towns adversely affected in all the unitary authorities created since the changes introduced following the Banham Commission. Within the metropolitan districts, there should be provision for all the towns which lost their civic identity in the 1974 reorganisation to claim enhanced town council powers (see above), if there is local support, irrespective of whether or not town councils are already in existence.

As suggested, different size criteria could be identified for the reallocation of different groups of services. This initiative would be feasible, gradual and modest in its cost implications. It would provide hope for Shrewsbury, Northampton, Barrow, Carlisle and Crewe and other real places which have disappeared from the local government map and for the many others which would suffer a similar fate if the unitary bandwagon were to roll on. And it would give substance to the reality that if we are to take the principle of subsidiarity seriously, we would need, in most parts of the country, a two-tier system of local government.

The appendix provides illustrations of the impact of our staged process of reform in three areas: Lincolnshire, Cumbria and Northamptonshire. It sets out in addition a provisional list of desirable changes in other parts of the country which would in total move us closer to the goal of a local government structure based on community identity and subsidiarity and our idea of local self-government, rather than technocratic 'bigger is better' assertions or ministerial whims.

Conclusion

As one wanders through the towns of England which have lost their civic identity, one is struck by the fact that almost always 'the town hall' is still there, whether gothic, classical or modern in design. Sometimes they are operating as area offices of the council into which the town has been incorporated, sometimes as headquarters of a town council, sometimes redeployed for some other use. But they are still there as symbols of a not-too-distant time in the past when local government was genuinely local and the residents of a town, through their local councils, were enabled to decide how the town should function, rather than such decisions being taken in some distant location. How wonderful it would be if such buildings once again became the focal points of the local community, busy with the day-to-day activity of local decision-making and bringing them physically closer to communities—a closeness which cannot be matched by modern technology or the internet. The circle would have again turned. As T.S. Eliot so eloquently put it 'time present and time past are both perhaps present in time future, and time future contained in time past'. In such a way local government would once again become truly 'local 'in nature, to the benefit of the citizens and communities it serves.

Reference

Jenkins, S. (2004). *Big bang localism.* Policy Exchange.

Appendix: How Devolution Based on Subsidiarity Might Work in England

All the proposals set out in this appendix are indicative in nature. They are included to illustrate a set of outcomes that would be consistent with and in the spirit of the move towards community-based local authorities advocated in Chap. 9.

They should all be subject to local referenda to establish whether or not local people wish to see powers restored to their town. The precise boundaries of the authorities concerned should be decided independently on the basis of journey-to-work catchment areas. We use three specific areas—Cumbria, Northamptonshire and Lincolnshire—to explain our approach and provide more general examples to illuminate the process we suggest.

Example One: Cumbria

- Barrow-in-Furness (plus remainder of Furness area) and Greater Carlisle (to be redesignated as unitary authorities).
- The remainder of Cumbria to operate as a rural region.
- Greater Workington, Whitehaven, Kendal and Penrith to be designated as (potential) municipal boroughs (Level One devolution).
- Egremont, Maryport, Cockermouth, Cleator Moor, Wigton, Keswick and Windermere/Bowness (plus any other former MB or UD with a population of over 10,000) to be designated as (potential) urban district councils (Level Two devolution).

S. Leach, C. Copus, *The Strange Demise of the Local in Local Government*, Palgrave Studies in Sub-National Governance,
https://doi.org/10.1007/978-3-031-32819-0

Example Two: Northamptonshire

- Northampton, plus its catchment area to the south and west (parts of Daventry DC and South Northamptonshire DC), to be designated as a unitary authority.
- North Northamptonshire to be combined with parts of rural Leicestershire and Cambridgeshire (west of the A1) to form a rural region.
- The remainder of West Northamptonshire to be combined with parts of Warwickshire and Gloucestershire (east of the M1) to form a rural region.
- Corby, Kettering and Wellingborough to be designated as (potential) municipal boroughs (Level One devolution).
- Daventry, Towcester and Rushden/Higham Ferres to be designated as (potential) urban district councils (Level Two devolution).

Example Three: Lincolnshire

- Greater Lincoln (including catchment area to the south west) to be designated as a unitary authority.
- Grimsby and its catchment area to be designated as a unitary authority, excluding the rural areas within North East Lincs to the north and east of the town.
- Scunthorpe and its catchment area to be designated as a unitary authority, excluding the rural areas within North Lincs which surround the town.
- The remainder of Lincolnshire to be designated as a rural region.
- Immingham, Gainsborough, Louth, Boston, Grantham and Skegness to be designated as (potential) municipal boroughs (Level One devolution).
- Sleaford, Spalding and Mablethorpe/Sutton-on-Sea to be designated as (potential) urban district councils (Level Two devolution).

Other possible developments consistent with our approach are as follows:

- Cheltenham and Gloucester and Worcester, where appropriate on extended boundaries, to become unitary authorities within a Mercia rural region to be designated embracing the remaining parts of Gloucestershire and Worcestershire.

- A new combined authority to be established linking Portsmouth, Southampton, Eastleigh, Havant and the intermediate areas. The remainder of Hampshire to be designated a rural region.
- A new combined authority to be established in the Calder Valley (Lancashire) linking Blackburn, Darwen, Hyndburn, Burnley (which could become a unitary authority), Nelson and Colne.
- Southport to be designated a unitary authority and detached from the Merseyside city region and combined authority. Formby to become part of the West Lancs rural region.
- Within West Yorkshire, Kirklees MBC to be divided into two smaller unitary authorities—Huddersfield and Dewsbury—and Wakefield MBC to be divided into two smaller unitary authorities—Castleford and Wakefield.
- Cheshire East unitary authority to be sub-divided into Greater Crewe and Greater Macclesfield unitary authorities, with its remaining territory designated a rural region and linked with rural areas to the west in Chester and West Cheshire UA.
- Lancaster and Morecambe to become separate (potential) municipal boroughs, with the remainder of the existing Lancaster Council area becoming part of the Cumbria/North Lancashire rural region.

Index

A

Abolition of the GLC, 29
Abolition of the metropolitan county councils, 29
Administrative convenience, 43, 45, 105
Average local authority size
  England, 4
  Scotland, 4
  Wales, 4

B

Barrow, 66, 67, 71, 78, 98, 104, 113, 120
Best Value reviews, 48, 50–54, 58
Boundary extensions (for city-based authorities), 114

C

Carlisle, 3, 16, 67, 69, 71, 78, 98, 104, 113, 120, 123
Civic engagement, 2
Combined authorities, 4, 44, 49, 62, 70, 71, 74, 80, 93, 97–99, 103, 110–115, 117, 118, 125
Communes (France), 6, 12, 23, 79, 87
Communities, 2, 5–7, 9, 10, 13, 14, 16, 21–25, 27, 28, 30, 44, 45, 56–58, 63, 64, 71, 72, 74, 78, 81, 91–93, 95, 97, 99, 101, 104, 110, 113, 115–119, 121, 123
Communities of place, 10, 62
Community identity
  affective, 3, 92
  effective, 3, 92, 93
Constitution (unwritten), 2
Cost-effectiveness and local authority size, 4, 20, 84, 88
Councillors
  accessibilty to public, 95
  councillor/population ratios, 13, 14, 45, 96
  workloads, 71, 91, 94–95

S. Leach, C. Copus, *The Strange Demise of the Local in Local Government*, Palgrave Studies in Sub-National Governance, https://doi.org/10.1007/978-3-031-32819-0

County boroughs, 10, 11, 22, 23, 26, 38, 78, 113, 118
County councils, 10, 11, 29, 31, 33, 50–52, 54, 55, 69, 70, 74, 92, 93, 97–103, 112, 113, 115
  different configurations of, 97
County-district relations, 48
Covid pandemic, 34, 43, 62, 65

D
De-localisation, 2, 17
Departmental opportunism (central government), 38, 43, 69
Departmental priorities (central government), 38
Department of Levelling Up, Housing and Communities (DLUHC), 4, 38
Devolution (within county councils), 32, 97, 99–103
Directly elected mayors, 32, 69, 80

E
Economic regeneration, 34, 39, 62, 63, 93, 97–99
Economies of scale, 6, 7, 21, 24, 28, 30, 44, 64, 72, 84, 87, 102–104
European comparisons
  councillor/population ratios, 13
  local authority size, 84
  prevalence of multi-tier local government, 78
Evidence-based analysis, 110

F
Failing authorities, 33, 34, 52
Football teams (as symbols of local identity), 12, 14–16, 101

I
Ideal size' for local authorities, 3, 87
Independent commissioners (in local government), 58
Indicators of democratic viability, 91, 97

J
Joint boards, 29, 80, 111, 112
Joint committees, 29, 55
Journey-to-work patterns, 93

L
Levelling Up' agenda, 5, 34, 39, 43
Local democracy, 2, 5, 7, 12, 45, 57, 63, 64, 84, 85, 89–99, 110, 116, 118, 119
  impact of move to bigger authorities, 27
Local government finance
  community charge (poll tax), 29
  council tax, 29
Local government reorganisations
  partial, 31–34
  system-wide, 20
Local government structure, 2, 10–14, 20, 22, 28, 29, 66, 78, 91, 102, 110, 113–115, 118, 119
Local identity, 6, 17, 31, 95
Local public participation, 90, 118
Lyons, Michael, 2, 15, 104

M
Morecambe Bay Authority proposal, 70
MPs/local party relationships, 50, 54, 55, 58, 65, 96, 97

Municipal boroughs, 10, 11, 13, 22, 26, 116, 117, 119, 123–125

N

Naming of shire districts
  ampersand, 27
  compass points, 27
  non-existent places, 27
Narratives of local government
  governmental, 5, 45
  technocratic, 5, 6, 62, 119
Neighbourhood empowerment, 39
Northamptonshire County Council
  changes in leadership, 52
  financial crisis, 7, 34, 58
  history of county-district relations, 48
  impact of reorganisation on community identity, 57, 113
  'Next Generation Council' strategy, 49, 51
  role of local MPs, 55
  transitional costs of reorganization, 56
  views of district council leaders, 53
Northern Powerhouse initiative, 32, 33, 39, 112

P

Parish councils, 11, 12, 68, 74, 84, 99, 100, 118
Party politics, 24, 96
Place shaping, 2, 3, 15, 44, 104, 119
Political salience, 6, 39
Public opinion surveys, 57, 68, 80

R

Relocalisation of local government, 115–121
Rules of the game, 41, 48
Rural district councils (RDCs), 11
Rural regions, 112, 114, 116–119, 123–125

S

Service delivery, 45, 62, 63, 69, 75, 84, 91, 119
'Social, economic and environmental well-being' power, 15, 44
Strategic planning, 44, 103
Strategic visions, 5
Subsidiarity, 11, 77, 78, 81, 111, 116, 118, 121, 123–125

T

Town councils, 99, 100, 116, 117, 119–121
Two-tier local government
  evidence of joint working, 114
  overlap and duplication, 74
  public confusion, 75

U

Unitary (all-purpose) councils, 5, 10, 31, 35, 39, 41, 63, 66, 72, 74, 76, 85, 105
Urban/rural distinctions and local government structure, 10, 12
Urban villages, 22